The author, who has a background of industrial sales and marketing, was responsible in the 1960s and 1970s for the marketing function of a division of a multi-million pound UK corporation. As such he spent periods in the 1970s in Eastern and Central Europe, usually when contracts were being finalised. This included Romania where the operating conditions for UK business visitors were made very difficult due to the grip that the then President, Nicolae Ceauşescu, had on the Romanian people, and the unethical business tactics that were employed in negotiations with Western business representatives The author experienced many of the difficulties presented at that time and it is around these that this story is based.

Charity Donation

The story is also based on the true situation at that time with regard to the forced policy of all married women under 40 years of age having to have 4 children, resulting in the creation of the orphanages. As a consequence of the injection of the children with infected blood, 53% of all children with aids in Europe are in Romania today. Because of this, the author is donating 50% of the royalties of the sale of this book to the charity, Children in Distress, which runs two hospices in Romania for the Romanian children with aids.

DO THEY KNOW ABOUT THE CHILDREN?

Ron Edmonds

*To John
Hoping that you enjoy the story! Ron.*

HAMWIC PUBLISHERS

Published by
HAMWIC PUBLISHERS
116 Woodlands Rd
Ashurst
Southampton
SO40 7AL, UK
Tel: 44 (0) 2380 292266; Fax: 44 (0) 2380 292382
http://www.hamwic.co.uk
email: enquiries@hamwic.co.uk

© Ron Edmonds 2004
ISBN 0-95472-281-7
Printed and bound in Great Britain by Antony Rowe, Eastbourne.

With the exception of the historical facts concerning the death of President Ceauşescu, late president of the Communist Republic of Romania, all events and places are fictional and any resemblance to persons, living or dead, is purely coincidental.

This book is sold subject to the condition that it shall not, by way of trade or otherwise, be lent, re-sold, hired out, or otherwise circulated without the publisher's permission in any form of binding or cover other than that in which it is published.

All rights reserved. No part of this publication
may be reproduced, stored or introduced
into a retrieval system, or transmitted in any form or by
any means without the prior permission of the publisher.

Dedicated to Bert Wing, work colleague and friend.

My grateful thanks to Alina Hughes for her guidance on the Romanian detail.

Prologue

In 1965, the megalomaniac dictator Nicolae Ceauşescu seized power and established the Socialist Republic of Romanian. He distanced the republic from Moscow and secured 'most favoured nation status' from countries like the US, which brought in economic aid from the West. Western nations, however, weren't completely aware of Ceauşescu's disastrous domestic policies. He impoverished the nation with grandiose projects like the 1000 room House of the People, the second largest building in the world. To pay off his country's debt he exported food while rationing necessities like meat and potatoes among his own citizens. Ceauşescu and his wife, Elena, lived in luxury leaving the Romanian people struggling to survive. Ceauşescu's desire to double Romania's population in one generation led to the tragic spectre of Romanian orphanages. During his rule, the law required that women have four children – later increased to five – by the age of 45, before they qualified for birth control or abortions. As poor families couldn't afford to raise them, turning children over to orphanages became an accepted part of Romanian culture. Eighty percent of the children in orphanages were of the Gypsy (Roma) race and were viewed as undesirables. Part of Ceauşescu's plan was that these impure children would be a pool of cheap labour for Romania.

In late 1989 the reign of terror ended. Father Laszlo Tokes, a beloved community figure, spoke out publicly against the dictator and was removed from his post by the Reformed Church of Romania, which was under Ceauşescu's control. This sparked angry demonstrations in Bucharest. Demonstrators were confronted with armoured tanks but the military, surprisingly, refused orders to fire on the people. Ceauşescu and his wife tried to flee Romania but were caught, tried and executed on December 23 1989.

By then there were more than 150,000 children in Romanian orphanages. News reports transmitted around the world showed images of malnourished children lying neglected in dirty cribs. Many of these toddlers, at the age of two and three, still hadn't learned how to talk or walk. Some were dying of infectious diseases. Romanian doctors had been forbidden to acquire medical information from other countries, thousands of children contracted HIV in a misguided attempt to improve their health through blood transfusions. As a result, half of Europe's AIDS-affected children, some 2300, are Romanian. One thousand children have already died from the disease in Romania. While orphanages in Romania have improved, the problem hasn't disappeared. At the time of writing there are currently 125,000 children in orphanages, as it's still considered an acceptable way for poor families to provide for their children. In fact, child abandonment has increased by 20 per cent since 1989.

PART I

Chapter 1

"Christ. Nothing seems to have changed."

The comment was really not addressed to anyone, but John the co-driver turned to David with questioning eyes.

"Sorry John, but it seems just the same as when I passed through here some fourteen years ago. I thought that with all the other changes this would have changed as well."

They had just passed through the friendly manned Hungarian border and were now confronted by a dark-blue-uniformed woman at the Romanian border post. Her attitude was far from welcoming.

David recalled the previous occasion when he passed through from the other direction, when he had been given the same unwelcoming attention.

"You have no prohibited items? No alcohol, cigarettes?"

"We have only the permitted bottle of Scotch per person and no cigarettes."

"You can leave one bottle here so that we can check it. We will return it to you after we have analysed a small sample."

No nothing had changed, thought David. Ceauşescu may be dead but the corruption lives on. Dutifully he handed over the duty-free bottle of Scotch, knowing full well that was the last he would see of it. After further scowls and poking inside the transit vans, they were beckoned through. David breathed a sigh of relief but wondered what else might hinder them in these new times. His thoughts went back to the events that had led him to Romania.

It was London, September 1967 and his day had been uneventful. As a technical rep for John Arkus, David had completed his planned number of calls. Some had been successful, others unsuccessful – much as usual. He thought that he had made some progress with John Carter who had promised him the next chance to quote for a conveyor belt for one of the pits in the Avery Sand and Gravel Group.

He'd made two courtesy calls on present customers. "Make sure your competitors don't start nibbling away at your hard won business," Alfred Tack had said on the Tack sales course he'd been put on by Arkus.

Driving home in his Morris Marina, it all seemed much of a sameness. OK it was a good job, he had a good boss – Reg Wilson was all right and Arkus wasn't a bad company to work for. It was respected as a supplier of industrial products, some they made and some they bought and sold.

He quite enjoyed the challenge of sales, making a bit of progress each year with the incentive of a little commission on his salary of £2400 a year. Although he wasn't really ambitious, he couldn't help thinking that he might still be doing this in five years' time.

He may get a promotion to Head Office, Product Manager or something, but who wants to live in Newcastle on the cold and windy Tyne?

David was quite proud of his achievements to date. After leaving his comprehensive school in Dagenham with only a few GCEs, he'd studied at evening classes at the local technical college and got his HNC in mechanical engineering. He'd secured a place in a small engineering company, which had eventually led to him getting a draughtsman's job at the great Dagenham plant of the Ford Motor Company.

As a presentable young man, now aged 25, he'd capitalised on his good looks and easy conversation with the opposite sex. He had played the local field of his choice of young women with quite some success, making sure however, that except for one, Sheila, the liaisons were short once a conquest had been made.

It had started to rain. He was on the North Circular, the Northern ring road round London that had been formed by joining up a number of roads in the 1930s, and it looked even more dreary as he made his way back to his home in Dagenham. He noticed that there was an irritating smear on the windscreen that the wipers seemed unable to clear. He brooded, and the more he thought the more he felt that some change was necessary if he were to continue to enjoy his working day.

He'd seen the advert in the London Evening Standard's classified columns:

```
Experienced sales person wanted to travel Eastern
Europe for company representing a number of well-
known principals selling industrial products. Write
in first instance to K.M. Industrial, P.O. Box 30.
```

He'd only been abroad once. It was a skiing holiday in Austria, with travel by train from Victoria Station. That had been exciting – until he fell on the nursery slopes on the second day and spent the next five days in the busy treatment rooms trying unsuccessfully to recover from a sprained ankle. Still, he'd enjoyed the atmosphere. He had even enjoyed the company of the waitress at the hotel. As with all the waitresses in the Tyrol she wore an Austrian dress with tight lacing under the bosom. Perhaps it was that that aroused him. In the short time before he resigned himself to the fact that he would not be able to ski again, he had been able to get a little further than just saying 'hello' in his broken German. Perhaps because she was experienced in dealing with the more amorous approaches of tourists, it progressed no further than a bit of cuddling and kissing. However, he had the opportunity to polish up his stuttering basic German.

On the other hand, Eastern Europe would be a very different matter. Here was a different way of life, or so he had read: with sombre Communist governments. Yet, it sounded exciting. An opportunity to see a bit of the world before he settled down – not that he had anybody in mind. Yes, there was Sheila but, of course, that was an attachment of convenience.

Perhaps it was a culmination of the weather, the humdrum of the past week and the thought that five years from now – in 1979 he would still be doing the same thing that spurred him on to put in an application for the job.

His present position required him to type a report every night This he usually put off, with the result that it often got posted with two other days' reports at the main post office in Barking, just in time to catch the last post.

Arkus provided him with an Imperial portable for this purpose, which was convenient if there was a need to produce an impressive job application. However, it took three attempts to get it right, and then only after slowing down on his scurry of fingers and thumbs that he usually applied to getting reports typed in time.

He'd almost forgotten about the submission when, some two weeks later, his mother brought a letter to him at the breakfast table. It was in the kitchenette of the council house where they'd lived for the last 27 years.

He knew that it was a reply on the job and looked at it for some little time, munching his toast, not daring to open it. He then realised that he had mixed feelings about the contents. Did he really want things to go further? It was a big step from his comfortable life with a doting mother who even cleaned his shoes every morning. Then there was Sheila, his receptive girlfriend of some considerable time, who responded so readily to relieve his hot-blooded passion. There were the lads too – those that were still out of the clutches of designing females – to have a drink with on a Saturday night.

With these misgivings, he tore open the flap.

```
K.M. INDUSTRIAL LTD
REPRESENTATIVES FOR INDUSTRIAL PRODUCTS
Mr David Edwards
15 Ledbury Rd
Dagenham
Essex

Dear Mr Edwards

We thank you for your letter of the 23rd August
1975 enclosing your curriculum vitae and we would
like to discuss this further with you in respect of
the present opening in our company for a sales
representative for our principals in the territory
of Eastern Europe.
```

```
Please confirm that you can present yourself for
interview at the Russell Hotel, Russell Square
London W.C. at 14.00 on Thursday 16th September.
Please telephone Mrs Blackmore to confirm.


P.J. Osbourne

DIRECTOR
```

The following day when David telephoned Mrs Blackmore she sounded distant and slightly haughty, but confirmed the appointment.

A whole week to wait. In that time he could hardly keep his mind off the thought of what he would do if he were offered the position. His mind had been wandering over the impending prospect of change, when once on the North Circular he'd nearly pushed the front of his Morris Marina into a braking car in front.

Visits to his customers took on a different air. Would he be going back there again? Would Arkus make any attempt to hold him? To make matters worse, McVitae and Price put in an enquiry for the PVC-nitrile conveyor belting order that he had been after for at least a year.

What about Mum? Would she miss cleaning his shoes, having his tea ready at any time of the evening he arrived home from his journey around the dreaded North Circular Road? And would he miss their shared times when they both had 'shut eyes' for twenty minutes or so by the coal fire in the early evening, before he returned to the life of a bachelor?

But wait a minute. He wasn't going to America; he would be back between visits. What had the advert said: 'travel to Eastern Europe', not live there.

The day of the interview arrived. He had never been in the Russell Hotel before. It struck him as a little out of touch with the times – there had been so many new hotels built in the past few years and by comparison with the President Hotel, which was close by, it was dated.

"Yes sir. What name?" asked the receptionist, looking at a list. "Mr Edwards? Ah yes, dear, here we are, 2 o'clock. That's what 1400 means doesn't it? I've never got used to talking about time in hundreds. Do take a seat over there, until Mrs Blackmore comes down for you."

Mrs Blackmore looked just as he'd imagined. About 45, glasses, hair straight back tied in a bun. If you were being kind, you'd say she was well rounded, but with a nondescript dress and an air of self-importance.

"Mr Edwards?" That wasn't an English accent. It was a little too staccato, clipped you might say. Although he wouldn't claim to be an expert on accents, he recognised it, of course. He'd heard the same kind of accent in Austria on the skiing holiday. She must be Austrian. But what about Mr Blackmore?

"Please come with me. Mr Osbourne can see you now." Of course, she could be married to an Englishman. David followed her up the ornate staircase to a large door, which led to a room with a high ceiling. At the end of the room were two men sitting at a dark polished table covered with green baize.

The taller of the two got up. "Come in Mr Edwards. Please sit down. This is Mr. Blackmore, my co-director." The mystery was now explained. He assumed that the first man was Mr Osbourne.

"Now, let's see. You are working with John Arkus at the present time."

"Yes sir."

Although times were changing and the way that people addressed their superiors was getting more relaxed, at John Arkus, which was traditionally directed by ex-military people, the more formal 'sir' approach was still used. He found it difficult to change. "I joined them five years ago."

Mr Osbourne smiled. "Tell us a little about yourself. What were you doing before that, for instance?"

He drew a deep breath and began the monologue presentation he'd practised in front of the mirror using his hands and shoulders to emphasise the points. (Alfred Tack had taught him in a sales course how you should bring attention to the important points of a presentation by the use of body language. Good old Alfred.)

He related how he had been a draughtsman, joined Arkus, had the six months' training course (this seemed to surprise them) and that he had been relocated to London after spending a period in the north, including time in cold and windy Newcastle-upon-the-Tyne.

However, he did recall that the girls were pretty there. Blonde too, perhaps a throw back to the days when the Vikings pillaged and plundered and then interbred with the locals in that part of ancient England. Not that he'd had much luck; perhaps it was his London/cockney accent that put the girls off.

He described his North London sales area, making the most of the successes he had had, emphasising the products that he'd sold to major companies.

"And what about your German?" asked Mr Osbourne after he had finished his piece.

"Ich spreche ein bischen Deutsch." David blurted out hoping that this wouldn't lead to a lengthy conversation. Following his start of German for his skiing holiday, he had taken up a chance to continue to learn from a warehouseman who worked at the London Depot of Arkus and his Austrian wife, Gretel.

Once a week he went to their two-room flat in Camden Town, enjoyed the 'Kuchen' that Gretel always made for his visits, then struggled to repay the dedication of the two of them by working hard to learn German. He'd learned Bismark's speech by heart and that often stood him in good stead when he wanted to impress.

"That's good," said Mr Osbourne. "German is a useful language for Eastern Europe. Now I suppose that you'd like to hear a little more about the position, but I must warn you we are seeing some others candidates for the appointment." David nodded.

"K.M. Industrial was founded by Mr Knowles and Mr Mathews just after the First World War when, due to the depression, there was an opportunity to represent companies in export areas. They chose Eastern Europe and were successful in getting the agencies for some emerging companies of that time, two of which were Krone Chemicals and Priory Paints, although they were not called that at that time; they are still with us today.

Unfortunately, Mr Knowles's only son was killed in the Second World War and he lost interest in the business and, after that it appears, in life itself. Mr Mathews never really took an interest in the business and I, together with Mr Blackmore, purchased the business in 1950. The business has successfully grown since that time. Of course, things have changed but there is still more business to be secured for our principals in the Eastern European area. But we need the right man if we are to expand our involvement."

"What about the Communists?"

"Their system of government is different from ours of course, but if one observes the rules there's no problem. Getting paid is difficult but that would not be your concern."

They went on to say that they already had one sales person, but he had found that the contacts were growing and that he needed to cut the size of his territory. So someone else was needed to cover Hungary and Romania.

Where exactly were Romania and Hungary? He had never thought about that part of Europe. He assumed that they had joint borders.

"How much time would I spend away?" he asked.

"Normally we would expect you to make a six-week visit and then you would have to follow that up by another six weeks in the office. Of course, there could be emergency visits if a contract was imminent. Harry has made quite a few of these recently to Romania. We don't encourage these because of the cost, but Harry has always been able to justify them by bringing back an enquiry."

Harry, he learnt, was Harry Robson the existing sales rep.

Not so bad, he thought. He might be able to keep things going with Sheila. Their relationship had been going on for some time; much of it had been in the back seat of the Morris Marina.

There was a little more discussion about when he would be able to start – the middle of November – and a request to supply names and addresses for references. He gave them two names. Roger, who had recently left Arkus to join Dunlop for one and Mr Gardner, who owned the little engineering fabrication company on the Rainham Road. He did some draughting for Mr Gardner, which kept his hand in, drawing up the fabricated drum reclaiming machines that Mr Gardner had designed and made for Barking Chemicals. It also gave him a little extra pocket money.

The interview ended and Mr Osbourne told him that he would be hearing from them by the end of the week.

True to their word, Friday morning saw the arrival of a business envelope.

"I bet it's from that firm dear," said his mother trying to hide her concern that it might be an offer. She stood by him while he opened it.

```
Dear Mr Edwards

Further to your interview on Thursday 16th
September 1975, we have pleasure in offering you
the position of Sales Representative for the
territory of Hungary and Romania at a salary of
£3000 p.a. plus expenses. You will be provided with
an Austin 1800 motor vehicle of which you will have
limited use to be agreed, when in England and the
use of another vehicle in Eastern Europe.

Initially you will spend the first week visiting
our two major principals, followed by three weeks
accompanying Mr Harry Robson whom will meet you in
Romania, assuming that you can start within four
weeks of the date of receipt of this letter.

Please confirm your acceptance of this position and
advise us of your starting date.

Yours sincerely

Peter Osbourne

DIRECTOR
```

"If you're going to benefit from changing your job, I suppose it's all right dear. You know what your dad always said, though: 'Think hard about leaving a good job and don't keep changing jobs'."

He had been at Arkus for five years. His dad had been a petrol tanker driver and had lived through the pre-war years of low employment. He had died soon after David had landed his reps job with a company car. His father had always been very caring and had worried about David's job situation.

He always regretted that his father hadn't lived a little longer so that he could have taken him out a little more. Although his father had died of pneumonia in 1967, he had been an invalid for many years, suffering from tuberculosis followed by restricted breathing problems.

It was time to broach the subject to Sheila.

"So I won't see you for six weeks at a time?" Sheila looked a little taken aback when he broke the news. David had always seen Sheila as a good-looking girl with a reasonable figure that he'd got know intimately over their two years together. Perhaps it was because of familiarity that he had never thought of her in any other way than as someone to fill the gaps between his other activities.

"It may not be for long." He tried to console her. "But it would give me a good experience for a sales manager's job."

He had a feeling that Sheila was a lost cause. Perhaps it was all for the good. One of Sheila's friends, trying to play cupid had once said, "When are you two going to get married?"

"Who'd marry either of us?" he'd replied. The remark had cost him her intimacy for two weeks!

"There'll be periods when we can be together in between the six week tours." He felt that he should make a final effort to retain contact. Sheila had always been a willing partner in the back of the Morris Marina. More as a gesture than with genuine hope, he added, "What about a cuddle in the back?". The pause that ensued made him fear that the damage had been done. Then he could feel Sheila relax and wriggle against him, with first one knee raised and then the other. The hasty disposal of her undergarment into her handbag indicated that he wouldn't leave without at least one more of her favours. The session on the back seat seemed to reach new heights for both of them, a culmination of many years of intimacy, intensified by the looming separation.

David lingered a little longer over his goodnight kiss, surprised to realise that it had stirred more feelings in him than before, but he quickly dismissed the thoughts.

The following day he broke the news to Reg Wilson. Reg looked a little taken aback and had made all the noises he expected before finally accepting the he'd be going. He had been a good boss. David was sure that Reg had known that something was in the air for a few days. David had been making an early finish on Fridays, but Reg had never taken him to task.

```
Dear Mr Edwards


Thank you for your acceptance letter. We look
forward to seeing you at Pentonville Road offices
on Monday 23rd October 1975 at 9.00 a.m. Please
find enclosed our official letter of employment.
```

Enclosed was the letter stating the expected duties and confirming the salary of £3000 p.a. and the pension after one year's employment. David wondered whether he would last that long; six weeks was a long time to remain celibate.

But hell! He was committed now. He would just have to keep his hot blood under control. His misgiving had gone now that he looked forward to the excitement of travel in a different country. No more of the stifling North Circular.

Chapter 2

David duly arrived at the office of K.M. Industrial, a plain set of offices on the second floor of a block in Pentonville Road, North London.

The offices occupied three separate rooms. One housed two young ladies and a young man about his own age or perhaps a few years older, say about twenty-six. It occurred to him that one of the women, who was quite attractive, was surreptitiously eyeing him up and down. Perhaps, he thought, the loss of Sheila may not after all mean a celibate life when he returned from his trips.

The middle office housed Mrs Blackmore. The more he looked at her, the more Austrian she looked: a little more rounded than when he last saw her, and her hair again tied back in a bun. The last office was that of Mr Osbourne. He learned that Mr Blackmore also travelled, his territory being Austria. So, that's where he'd met Mrs Blackmore. Perhaps it would be possible for him to meet someone too, perhaps a little more attractive, who could make him want to give up the nights out with the boys, the hunts for other conquests, and settle for a life with just one girl?

"Come in David. You don't mind if we call you that do you. Good. Now, sit down. I've drawn up a programme for you for your visits, but first you will be spending two days with our office people. We will initially send you for training and information on the product ranges of just the two main principals: Krone Chemicals and Priory Paints. After the first trip you can do a quick round of the other smaller accounts we handle."

It had been arranged for him to spend two days in each of the companies: Krone Chemicals in Bedford and Priory Paints in Silvertown, East London. He knew the latter because he had often passed the Works when, as a boy, his father had taken him out for a day in his petrol tanker to fill up at the distribution centre.

What would his dad have said if he knew that, some twenty years after those schoolboy rides in the Scammell tanker, he would be travelling the same streets in pursuit of foreign travel? Suddenly he missed not having his father to share the excitement he now felt.

The rest of the day he spent first with Mrs Blackmore, learning how to fill in reports and expense claims, and then with the young man – Jimmy Jones – who received the orders and processed them. To his pleasure, he also had a seat by the prettier of the two ladies, the one who had shown interest at his arrival; David estimated that she was in her mid-twenties.

Her name was Ingrid and she was German, although you would not have guessed from her perfect English accent. She had recently come from Osnabrück, which he later found out was towards the north of Germany. Definitely a possibility, he thought. However, he would have to wait until he got back from his first trip to pursue a more intimate relationship. However, by the end of the day he was already fantasising about what might be, substituting the image of Sheila for that of Ingrid.

He was to spend his first two days with Priory Paints.

"So you've joined K.M. have you?" This was his contact, Mr Palmer, the export administration manager, who was housed in a rather old-fashioned office reached by stone steps from the entrance. The office, he thought, matched the age and outside state of the building.

"They've been associated with us for many years, I believe they took on the agency just after the war."

"Yes," David answered and recounted the little bit of history that he gleaned at his job interview. It seemed to impress Mr Palmer.

"Well if you do as well for us as Mr Robson has, we'll be pleased. He's got us some good contracts for our metal paint products as well as a steady flow of sales of the general paints. He seems to know just when to make a trip. Sometimes he makes special trips, which we wouldn't normally encourage – we get invoiced for his expenses you know, but he always returns with a good enquiry and some guidance as to how we should price the tenders."

David made assurances that he would do his best.

What if he didn't come up to Harry Robson's standards, he thought. He set about getting all the information, which he thought would allow him to make the best presentation to the foreign companies. "Know your product," Alfred Tack had said. Tack's sales training course had stood him in good stead for five years. He hoped it wouldn't let him down now.

He took in all the information: catalogues, technical notes, samples, tests, mixing standards, anti-ageing additives. At the end of the second day he felt prepared to talk about the products with an element of confidence.

It seemed strange to be getting the bus to Camden Town station, passing along the same streets that seemed unchanged since he had been driven down them in his father's Scammell.

The second trip was to Bedford. He had never been there before, but then he had hardly really been anywhere in England.

Krone Chemicals was different. It had a modern office block, beside what appeared to be a complex and highly technical plant. The company was an offshoot of a Swedish company that had acquired the original firm some ten years previously: hence the modern offices and furnishings. They were market leaders in the UK for additives for the plastic and rubber processing trade. They supplied Dunlop among others. That appeared to be a coincidence – Roger having gone from Arkus to Dunlop.

David couldn't help noticing that many of the girls were Latin looking, with dark hair and slightly sallow skins. Then he remembered someone telling him that many of the Italian prisoners of war had settled there after the war, working in the London Brick Company. Obviously the genes had carried down the generations. They were not his type though. His thoughts turned to Ingrid who was more accessible. He had already found out that she lived at Manor Park, East London, only three underground stations from Beacontree, the station

16

within walking distance of his mother's house. Until her interest in a closer relationship was confirmed, he would direct his winning techniques in that direction.

The two days at Krone were spent hectically learning about the products and their advantages over the competition. He had the impression that the company was intensively driven. Every one he met appeared to be a 'company person', or tried to give that impression.

It was a different world from the close working relationships that he had experienced with Arkus. Reg Wilson, although a good manager, had been an open sort of person and, in retrospect, life there seemed uncomplicated. At Krone Chemicals, he felt an atmosphere of competitiveness between the employees. Perhaps this was the real business world. He took comfort from the fact that he had made the move – a chance to gain some experience that would stand him in good stead for an entry into sales management.

He returned to the office in Pentonville Road the following week. Ingrid seemed noticeably more interested. This was confirmed when he was sitting beside her, learning how the invoices and bank documents were prepared.

They'd just gone through the order routine when she asked if he was married. "No," he said and went on to add that when he met Miss Right, he felt sure that he would be happier than he was now as a lone bachelor. It was, of course an engaging lie, but it worked! The vibes were definitely there. He suggested that when he returned from his first trip he could meet up with her to learn a little more about how things worked. He felt sure that she understood when their bodies 'accidentally' brushed each other as they moved around the filing cabinets.

"Well David, I'm afraid that will have to do for the moment." Mr Osbourne showed a little concern. But then his rather formal manner relaxed a little. "However, you'll have Harry to look after you. He's travelling over to Bucharest from Budapest." That was from Hungary, David thought. They seemed to be able to drop the names of these cities as if they were stations on the Upminster to Charing Cross underground.

"Harry will show you how to handle the Romanians, and on the next trip you'll both be back in Hungary."

There was a further discussion of the details of his journey. David was to set off on a Saturday night and was booked in at the Aerial Hotel by Heathrow airport. He remembered passing it on his travels with Arkus; it looked like a big pork pie. On the Sunday morning he would catch the SwissAir flight to Zurich and from there he would catch the Tarom – the Romanian National airways – flight to Bucharest. He would be met at the airport by Harry, who would take him to the Theodore Hotel. It irritated David that Mr Osbourne pronounced it Theodoor.

There was one Friday night left before he had to leave! Normally he put Sheila on hold at the weekend and played the field with the boys. When he wasn't successful at the Palais, there was always Mary to fall back on. She would wait patiently, almost like a puppy, until he asked her for a dance, having failed to 'pull' anyone else, and then agree to be taken home in the Marina for a kiss and cuddle and a bit of petting in the car. He hoped that this could be improved upon, but he was taking his time.

However, this time he thought that the conditions would be more favourable if he were to suggest to Sheila that they had an evening together. Her co-operation, when they'd returned to her bed-sitter, where they were able to extend their activities that were normally restricted by space in the back of the Marina had left them both breathless. He was surprised at Sheila's new-found largess and, reflecting on this seemed to shorten the train journey the next day from Beacontree to Heathrow.

"Are you sure that you've enough clothes dear?" his mother had said anxiously as he left. He couldn't help smiling at her doting attention. He remembered how she'd cried when he limped into their council house a week early on his return from the Austrian skiing holiday with a badly sprained ankle. Mothers were funny he thought. They get so little reward for all the affection they lavish on their offspring.

He made himself a promise to make more effort to show her how much he appreciated her when he returned.

Chapter 3

The Aerial Hotel near London Heathrow Airport was very smart and typically American. The meal in the restaurant was without character – tasteless steak and a cold sweet. The room was carefully planned so that everything took up as little space as possible. Oh, well, he was only staying overnight and there was a whole new world ahead – literally. After the meal, there was nothing else for him to do but to go to the bar or go back to his room. He explored the bar and found it sparsely furnished with what appeared to be uncomfortable seats, so he opted for his room. Although everything was concertinaed, he had noticed that, tucked away in the top corner, there was a small television. With a bit of luck he might be able to watch 'Match of the day'.

Much as he enjoyed football, the television lulled him to sleep. He suddenly woke finding himself on the bed with the T.V. still on, but now it was well past the end of the programme. He got undressed and slipped between the sheets and was soon fast asleep

An early morning call woke him with a start. Breakfast had been planned for 7:00 p.m. in order to catch the hotel courtesy bus to the Airport. He hurriedly showered in the cramped bathroom, shaved and dressed, and made his way down, via the lift, to the breakfast room.

Once there, he noticed that there were only a few other guests taking breakfast. Besides woman-watching, one of his pastimes was trying to guess where people came from. He could bore a listener for hours on how Scotsmen held their mouths on the side, and the reason for the straightness of the nose on 'Brummies' who, although always very friendly, spoke with their back teeth clenched. He amused himself with this pastime while waiting for breakfast to arrive. Surely, he thought, that man over there is an American. Yes, he eats with his fork, using his knife only to cut his bacon into smaller pieces. The one thing David's father had been strict about was teaching him to use his knife and fork properly. It always gave him confidence whenever he was entertaining customers to know that he had good manners.

Another man had ashen skin, and looked like some of the boys after six pints on a Saturday night after the dancing was done. One other diner was obviously from a Latin country: dark skinned with black hair. There were no women, he noticed. Well, you can't have everything!

Breakfast over, he paid the bill. What! That much, he thought. Then his apprehension died when he remembered that he didn't have to settle the bill; it was all down to K.M. Industrial.

The courtesy bus dropped him at Terminal 2, which dealt with passengers for flights other than BEA. He checked in at the SwissAir desk and passed all his luggage through at the check-in. There was no need to hold on to his briefcase as it contained only his product sheets and a notebook.

There was still time to look around. Should he buy a duty-free bottle? No one had briefed him on the customs regulations at Bucharest. Surely they'd let you take in at least one bottle. Why not take advantage of the special offer and take two half-litre bottles of the Teachers. He'd been told to take cigarettes – apparently the brands in Romania smelled terrible and tasted as if they'd been made out of old car tyres.

He had just finished collecting and paying for this duty-free when he noticed that, on the departure board, the SwissAir flight to Zurich was flashing 'Boarding Gate 19'. He couldn't help feeling excited as he searched for Gate 19. There was the ashen-faced man also making his way to the same gate. So was the Latin-looking chap; perhaps he was a Romanian.

The charming manner of the SwissAir hostess made him feel as if he was going on holiday. "Seat 23? Half way down on the right sir." Good, he had a window seat. He wasn't a newcomer to flying; he'd been on a couple of package holidays, but this was different. As he walked along the aisle he couldn't see the sea of faces crammed in as there had been on the package flights. This was more spacious, and there was not the babble of excited voices that he had come to accept on the holiday flights.

David passed the ashen-faced man, but the Latin chap must have been further on. Fastening his seat belt, he noticed that he could stretch out his legs. That was also a bit different from the charter flights.

He was soon joined by a man in a business suit who, once he had put his briefcase in the upper locker, smiled and offered a greeting. David didn't know whether to say anything or to wait until his travelling companion started a conversation. To his relief the stranger approached him.

"Looks as if we will be leaving on time."

"Yes," and then, taking advantage of their conversation, he added, "So that means I shouldn't have any trouble with my connecting flight to Bucharest?"

"I shouldn't worry about that," he replied. "Most of the people on board are catching that flight. I would think that Tarom would hold the plane."

He remembered that Tarom was the airline that he was taking – Romanian State Airways.

"Are you connecting for Bucharest?" Here was a chance to get a little more information on the procedures.

"Yes, for my sins. I make the trip about four times a year," he replied. "The sooner in and out the better."

David felt a slight apprehension that began to tighten his chest.

"It's my first visit," he blurted out. Why he had said that he didn't quite know: perhaps to get some support from this stranger. It had crossed his mind that, although they were in talking quite socially, he didn't know his companion's name, nor perhaps would he.

It was a quirk of the British, he thought, not to rush immediately into introductions. Not like Americans whom he'd met who wanted to force your name out of you by introducing themselves and their wife, and tell you how many children they had and where they lived. If encouraged, they'd bring out their wallets to show you photos of the kids within two minutes of striking up a conversation.

"'Been briefed?" The stranger's face suddenly reflected some concern.

"Well, not really, but I'm meeting a colleague at the airport – Harry Robson." He posed the question but because his companion did not respond to the name, he assumed that he didn't know him.

"You'll have to meet him outside the customs area." He looked thoughtfully up at the ceiling of the aircraft.

"Even if you've been to other Commicon countries, there are a few things that you ought to know about our friends in Romania."

"I've only ever been to Austria," David replied, "and that was on holiday." He felt a tinge of remorse when he remembered how unsuccessful that had been, especially the twisted ankle.

"Look, let me point out a few things that may be helpful."

David realised that he was only too willing to hear anything that would help him.

"You ought to remember that Ceauşescu rules Romania with a rod of iron." For a moment David was not able to place the name. Then he remembered that Ceauşescu was the Communist president of Romania.

"Control by the state is stronger in Romania than in any other Eastern European bloc country, even perhaps stronger that in the USSR. Step out of line and you could be in deep trouble. But I suppose your colleague, Harry Robston, will tell you that."

He felt like correcting him on the name, but didn't want to disturb the flow of information.

"The first thing you'll experience is passport control. Expect to be scrutinised. Don't look anywhere but straight at the officer, and smile. He will be sitting behind a high counter in his little box and whilst you're standing there he is looking through the list of names in quite a big document. I don't know how big it is because you can't see it. I can tell you that when I made my first trip, some years ago now, I felt quite worried. What exactly they are hoping to find I don't know, but it can be an unpleasant experience.

Then you will go through customs. If you're thinking about looking for the green channel, forget it. There is only one route through customs and whether you are here for the first time or you have been before, you will have to open your bags: even your briefcase." He paused and then looked even more concerned. "You haven't any confidential papers in your brief case have you?"

"No," David replied.

"Good. Although I don't think that the idiots at the customs would be able to distinguish between those and the price lists. I would expect to lose something."

"Lose something?"

"Yes. At this visit I always bring about 10% more diaries than the number that I need to give out to my contacts because I know that that is roughly the number that will be missing when I open my case at the hotel. Where are you staying, by the way?"

"At the Theodore." David pronounced it 'Theodoor', the way Mr Osbourne had. It was obviously correct because his companion had made no comment.

"That's OK. A little 1920s, but OK. I'm at the Corinthian Palace." "Then," continued his companion, "you come to the changing of your money. You've got travellers' cheques I suppose?"

"Yes," he replied, "they didn't give me any Romanian money."

"That's because there's none available in the West. You aren't allowed to take any Romanian money out of the country, but you will be told how much you must change by the change people. You'll find their window outside the customs area."

What do you mean, 'told'?" Surely, he thought, they couldn't tell me what, or what not, to change.

"You're stopping until Friday?"

"No, I'm here for two weeks."

"Well, they will ask you how long you are staying and, according to the days, you will have to change a minimum of so much per day. Your hotel bill is paid?"

"Yes I have a voucher for the two weeks, or rather I have a voucher for one week at the Theodore and another voucher for any other hotels that I may use. I believe that we will be going out of Bucharest."

"Then they will make you change at least £10 per day for each day that you are in Romania. You can change more but not less. Remember, you can't take any Romanian money out and there are problems if you want to change any money back into pounds."

It was all getting a little complicated he thought and he said as much.

"Well, it's their way of making sure you don't buy any money on the black market."

Now things were *really* getting complicated, he reflected.

"This brings me to another point, although I'm sure that Harry Robston will cover this." (David resisted the thought of correcting the name.) You are sure to be approached at some time, possibly in the street or a restaurant if you have to dine out of the hotel." Have to dine out of the hotel? Have to? This was getting ridiculous.

"You will be asked if you have any currency to sell and you will be offered a better exchange rate than the official 25 Lei to the pound."

"Why would they want to do that?"

"Because they can make a profit on the resale and also because there is no other way that anyone can get their hands on Western currency. In Romania things can be bought for hard currency that cannot be bought using local currency. Also, when people are able to travel out of Romania – on trade missions and the like – they can buy things that are not available in Romania."

"It seems worth cashing in on." David thought that he was showing a little entrepreneurial spirit.

"At your peril! There are two dangers in getting involved. One – if you get caught you will end up being detained by the Communist police; and two – the person you are dealing with could be a police informer."

It had all sounded a bit dramatic, Reds under the bed sort of thing.

He didn't want to offend his travelling companion, so he made no comment except to thank him for the information.

The in-flight breakfast arrived. This was different from what he had imagined: hot bacon and scrambled egg with real stainless steel knives and forks.

He learned during further conversation that his companion worked for himself and came to Romania to buy Romanian country clothing that he sold to retailers around the world. He bought country clothing from other Eastern European countries too but, because of the gypsy influence in Romania's history, he found a ready market for the Romanian style of clothing. He obviously knew his way around.

The meal over and the trays cleared, the announcement came over the address system that they were approaching Zurich. David never quite lost the excitement of seeing the plane come in over the approaching landscape. Switzerland wasn't quite so interesting as Austria but then Zurich is a commercial and industrial city, not a Tyrolean holiday resort.

The landing completed, he made his way out of the aircraft and down the steps to follow the other passengers into the transit bus.

On arriving in the transit terminal, he found that he had to wait about three-quarters of an hour for the call for the ongoing connection. Rather than continue his conversation with his recent travelling companion, he found a corner where he could quietly reflect on the information he had given him. "It couldn't really be like that could it?", he thought. At least he would have Harry Robson to show him the ropes.

The call came to board and the indicator confirmed that the Tarom flight TAR 452 to Bucharest was boarding from Gate 7. Again, he was required to board the transit bus and this time he was taken out much further from the terminal.

On alighting from the bus, he was herded with the rest of the passengers to an area by the side of the aircraft. This was a Russian-made Ilyushin 18, and he was asked to identify his bags for loading on to the aircraft before he was allowed to board up the steps. This was a security measure, he was told, to ensure that no strange baggage entered the aircraft.

Various owners were pointing out their bags and David waited and waited until eventually the last bags had been claimed, but he couldn't see his bag and brief case. He found himself the only passenger on the tarmac without any bags.

"Your baggage must have been mislaid," the rather dark-skinned official said to him. "You can go on to Bucharest and wait for them to arrive on the next aircraft." No, the official insisted, he couldn't wait for somebody to go back to the terminal and check.

"If you don't want to come on this flight, you can take the flight this evening to Constanta and get the train tomorrow morning to Bucharest. But we must close the flight now." He had no idea where Constanta was, but the thought of not having his catalogues, let alone all his clothes, made him decide to stay and try to locate his baggage.

He boarded the bus again and was taken back to the terminal building. There he was taken to the SwissAir information desk where he explained his position. The official, who seemed to treat all this as an everyday occurrence, asked him to wait by the desk. After some ten minutes, another uniformed SwissAir steward arrived and asked David to follow him to the baggage compound.

Once there it was easy to identify his baggage. "Why it wasn't transhipped, I don't know," confessed the SwissAirman, "but that's Tarom for you. You'll have to go through customs again, so follow me and I will explain the situation on the exit channel." He picked up his bag and briefcase and only then noticed that one of the catches was broken. The other, although closed, was unlocked. He was sure that he had locked both of them. He supposed that they had been subjected to the notorious handling by the baggage men.

Once through customs, he again found the SwissAir desk. It transpired that SwissAir were the agents for Tarom and that there was only one Tarom official based at the airport. He suspected that that was the official he'd seen when he got off the aircraft.

Having explained the position, the official made a search through flight papers and finally advised him that there was a Tarom flight scheduled for 21.30 to Constanta and that he could be booked on that.

Yes, a telex could be sent to the Theodore Hotel advising them of his delayed arrival. Yes, they would ask the hotel to pass a copy to a Mr Harry Robson advising him of the change and informing him that David would make his own way to Bucharest and the Theodore Hotel. (Heaven knows how he was going to do that, he thought.)

He would be given free meal vouchers for the Airport restaurant, courtesy of S.A/Tarom. With this all settled, he surrendered his baggage again, this time retaining his briefcase.

The meal in the restaurant gave him another chance to people-watch. There was something about airports that was rather mystical. He tried to guess where everyone was going. There were a few people who were obviously dressed for skiing. It was still only November, though. Well, he supposed that there could be snow in France or even Austria at that time of year. He'd been skiing in December, over the New Year.

He remembered how, on New Year's Eve in Saalbach in the Tyrol, it had been wonderful to see the experienced skiers coming down the mountain, all holding candles. By that time he was already suffering from his twisted ankle. It occurred to him that at least he had the memory of his abortive attempt to emulate those skiers. "Always try to remember things," his father had drummed into him as a young boy. "You'll be able to enjoy your memories when you're older." It was true. He looked back on many of the things that had happened in his childhood with some pleasure. It was funny how many of the things that his father had said had, at the time, seemed pointless. Was it the insecurity of his present predicament that had made him now reflect on their relationship just now?

Time seemed to drag and he exhausted all the diversions. He had just finished a second meal at the restaurant when, thankfully, the flight indicator had showed Flight TAR 345 to Constanta Gate 7 – the same gate as before.

He followed the signs to Gate 7 and arrived there some minutes later only to find that he was the only one there. Perhaps he had been a little quick in responding to the call, he thought. Five minutes passed and he was still the only person sitting in the empty boarding room. He watched the clock as it came passed 21.30 and reached 21.35 and decided that it was time to make some enquiries.

Trundling back to the SwissAir information desk he found that there was a different girl on the desk. Well it had been over ten hours since he first got to the desk. However, this one was perhaps even more attractive than her predecessor.

The girl didn't look in the least perturbed and immediately picked up the phone, advising that she would check with the Tarom representative – our dark-skinned friend – to find out the position.

After what appeared to be an endless wait, she put the telephone down. "He has obviously gone home," she said, this time looking a little put out. "I'll check with Bucharest direct. Can I suggest that you take a seat, it may take some time to get through?"

What the hell was going on? David thought. No flight, no representative, it was ridiculous. After a further 20 minutes – time was beginning to drag now – she called him back to the desk.

"I'm afraid that that flight has been cancelled."

"You mean it didn't even leave Romania? But how can it be announced as leaving from Gate 7?"

Unflappable, she said in a resigned voice, "The Tarom representative advises the SwissAir flight people working with them on the Tarom flights that the flights are going out each day. I suppose that because the representative is not here to advise otherwise, the announcement system goes on automatically.

"There is a flight for Bucharest tomorrow at 14.00. We can book you on that." The thought of dossing down in the airport terminal until 2 o'clock the next day appalled him.

"We will arrange for overnight accommodation at the Zurich Hilton." David was beginning to wonder how he would explain all this additional cost to K.M.

"Of course all the cost will be billed to Tarom." She smiled at this point – for the first time – as if she were enjoying billing them for their inefficiency.

After arranging for further telexes to be sent to the hotel and Harry Robson, tired and a bit dejected, David was about to make his way to the courtesy bus stop to board the bus for the Hilton, when he noticed the SwissAir girl still looking at him. Surely not! It was worth a try.

"And what time do you get off duty Miss…?"

There was a smile again and then, "Neumann, Ingrid and 22.30." The slight Swiss accent was now noticeable.

"You have been so kind, I would like to buy you a drink if you are going past the Hilton on your way home." It was a different line from 'Do you come here often?', frequently used at the Ilford Palais, but it worked.

"I would like that." The smile was still there. "I will see you in the bar at the Hilton at, say about a quarter to eleven. Now you should hurry or you will miss the bus."

David suddenly felt much better.

True enough, he was booked into the Hilton. The room, much larger than that at the Aerial, had a tea-making machine, some fruit and a small 'fridge, which, when he explored the contents, he found to contain some bottles of beers and some miniatures, gin, whisky, brandy etc.

So Tarom will be billed, eh! David enjoyed the gin and tonic even more, knowing this was being billed to Tarom. Then he showered and put on the clean shirt that he had wisely stuffed into his overnight bag.

True enough, Ingrid was in the bar when he got there. She had changed out of her uniform and had a pastel blue blouse under a soft linen jacket. It set off her blonde hair and also, as he was quick to notice, her neat bust.

"Hello David." She had obviously looked at his booking details. "How is the room?"

"Very nice. But can I get you a drink?"

"Don't you have a mini-bar in your room?"

"Well yes…"

"Since Tarom are paying, why don't we use that?" With that, she got up from the sofa and looked meaningfully at David and then towards the elevator.

The three-floor ride up in the elevator was made in silence but when the doors opened Ingrid took David's hand.

"Give me your key."

Looking down at the number, Ingrid turned towards the appropriate room, still holding his hand and releasing it only to put the key in the lock. Once inside she placed the key on the small bedside table and went to the mini-bar.

"I'm having a vodka and coke, what do you want David?"

Still a little overcome by the speed of events, David answered: "Gin and tonic would be fine."

Glasses filled, she once more took his hand and lead him to the sofa.

" So tell me how you come to be going to Bucharest?"

Her wide blue eyes were more that a little distracting. However, he managed to piece together the events and maintain a little control over himself.

" What about you? Do you travel with SwissAir?"

" I hope to, but I have to have a spell behind the desk before I can get on the training course for a hostess position."

The drinks were nearly finished when Ingrid got up.

"Do you mind if I use your bathroom?"

"Be my guest." All of this was a bit out of David's league and he really didn't know whether or how he should progress. The decision was made for him when Ingrid emerged from the bathroom minus the blouse and jacket that she had gone in with. The lingerie was pale blue and very, very feminine. Walking over to the bed, she turned down the covers and slipped underneath.

" Let's see if you will sleep well tonight. Coming in?"

The events that followed certainly helped him to sleep and he was surprised to see that it was after 8 o'clock when he woke. To his disappointment, he found that he was alone. He wondered whether he had dreamed the whole thing, but his nakedness confirmed that that was not the case. His first thought was whether he should get up quickly and get over to the airport terminal. Then he remembered that he wasn't flying out until 2 o'clock in the afternoon.

Enjoying the luxury of the room, he made himself a pot of tea, then showered and shaved, marvelling at the splendid bathroom. The room was comfortably warm; the central heating allowed him to walk about semi-naked. This was a bit different from the council house back in Dagenham; the only heating there was a coal fire, which was kept in night and day in the living room.

He sauntered down to breakfast, which was buffet style, and ensured that he had a sample of everything. It surprised him to see the cold meats and cheese, but there was also hot bacon and scrambled egg.

Once breakfast was over, David decided that it might be prudent to get back to the Terminal to ensure that he was in time for the flight. Catching the courtesy bus and clutching bag and briefcase, he arrived at the Swissair information desk again. The first girl was back on duty again. He wondered if he should ask about Ingrid but decided that that might compromise her, so he decided to say nothing.

"Hello sir." She was about the same age as him so it sounded strange.

"I heard of the problem with the 21.30 flight. It's happened before. Still I see from the copy here that you've advised your hotel in Bucharest. You had better have that." She passed over the slip of paper. "You're booked in on the 14.00 flight, I see. Well, we will be calling that about 13.20, so you can take a snack at the restaurant if you like." She passed over a meal voucher similar to those that that he had previously been given. At this rate he was going to pile on the weight, he thought. Not good for the image! He decided to miss the snack.

True enough, at 13.20 the flight was called and he duly trundled along to Gate 21 where, to his relief, there was a whole crowd of people waiting. At last, the stewardess announced that they could board and, with a bit of shoving from some of the passengers, he filed into the aircraft and took his seat.

The aircraft was similar to that in which he'd flown from Heathrow. After the seat belt check, the stewardess had returned to her seat and, within minutes, they were on their way. This time his companion was not so talkative and it was well into the two-hour journey and after the meal had been served that he first spoke.

"We seem to be on time." Perhaps just an icebreaker remark. "Do we?" David queried.

"'Should just about get down before dark. But I suppose we will be held up at the airport as usual. Where do you usually stay?" he asked. He had obvious guessed that David was a business traveller, but then from what he heard from the other travelling companion, no one in their right senses would go to Bucharest on holiday.

"I am booked in at the Theodore Hotel."

"I'm at the Intercontinental. I used to use the Theodore but it's a bit old fashioned for me. The Intercontinental's an improvement if you don't mind the stereotype American type décor," replied his companion.

The announcement had come over the p.a. system that they were about to land. He looked out of the window and could see Otopeni Airport, Bucharest, below. He was surprised to see a large number of soldiers; at least he thought that that they were soldiers. They certainly carried rifles but they looked rather scruffy in their ill-fitting khaki greatcoats. Even when the aircraft came to a halt there were still a host of soldiers on the tarmac.

"It seems as if we've come in at a special time," he said to his companion.

"Eh? Oh the army. That's normal. You've obviously not been here before. Don't worry, that is just to ensure you don't slip in by any other way than through immigration."

It seemed a long time before the doors opened. From the top of the aircraft steps he was able to see the entrance to the terminal perhaps 100 to 150 yards away. However, to his surprise they were herded into transit buses that closed their doors and stood, without moving, for what had seemed an interminable time.

"Why do we have to take the buses?" he asked his flight companion who, happened to be standing besides him.

"Because somebody decided that they should have transit buses and therefore they've got to be used." It seemed a strange explanation.

Eventually the bus started and almost immediately the doors at the entrance to the airport terminal opened. Another soldier, complete with an automatic rifle, was stationed at the entrance. Why such a military presence? he thought.

He followed the other passengers through the corridor and into the passport control area. As had been explained to him, he was required to pass over his passport at the high-countered little box of an office. All he could see was the head and shoulders of the immigration officer, this time dressed in a blue uniform. He remembered the advice of his fellow traveller from Heathrow. "Smile." A fixed smile was conjured up as he looked at the immigration officer who looked down at something, then looked up and then looked down again. 'Surely this is a joke,' he thought, only to realise much later that that was another big mistake. Two more upward looks and then his passport was returned without a word.

Making his way through to the baggage collection, he found his bag and passed on to customs. No, there was no green stream. Placing his bag on the counter as everyone seemed to be doing, he waited his turn to be processed. After what appeared to be an eternity, another blue-uniformed man appeared alongside his bag. He ignored David. Then, with a very hostile expression, he looked up.

"What is the purpose of your visit?" the English was clipped.

"Business," David answered. "I am visiting some of your companies."

"Which ones?" Panic. He didn't know the full itinerary. "Er. My colleague, who's already arrived, knows the visiting programme."

"And you don't?"

"Sorry, not yet, but he is waiting for me outside."

"And how long are you staying?" Ah, he was able to answer that: "Two weeks."

"That's just my library book," explained David as his blue-uniformed friend found the Neville Shute paperback and checked that there was nothing loose between the pages. He looked at the catalogues of Krone and Priory Paints. He then noticed the two half bottles of duty-free whisky. He took one out and put it to one side.

"You can fasten your bag." David was just about to reach for the half bottle when he remembered the conversation. "Expect to lose something."

"You will need to change your travellers' cheques before you leave the airport." He was shown by a wave of the hand to move on.

Having gone out through the double doors, he looked anxiously for a sign that would identify Harry Robson. He was supposed to hold up the Krone catalogue. There weren't many people waiting and certainly no catalogue was being held up. Perhaps he was delayed, he thought. He decided to get his money changed and wait a little. A window in the far wall had the sign 'Change' over it. He went over and again an unsmiling man interrogated him.

"How many days are you in Romania?" "Fourteen," he replied.

"You have hotel vouchers?" David nodded. "You will change £140." David only had travellers' cheques made up to the value of £150.

"That will do and you will change any remaining Lei back when you leave." He received 3675 Lei. The little piece of brownish paper said that he had been given 25 Lei to the pound and charged 2% commission.

Moving away from the change window, he decided to wait a little longer. Although he had a good view of the airport reception area, there was no sign of any Krone catalogue being held up. Twenty minutes had passed when he was approached by a khaki-uniformed official.

"Why are you waiting?" The question was blunt and in clipped English. He explained that he was waiting for his colleague, Harry Robson of K.M. Industrial, and would be visiting some businesses in Bucharest.

"This Mr Robson. Why is he not here?" David was beginning to feel a little uncomfortable now.

"I'm sorry I don't know. He was supposed to meet me here from the flight. Perhaps he has been delayed."

"You will come with me." It was not a request but an order, and he noticed that the official had his hand on his revolver attached to his leather belt. Dutifully accompanying him to a door at the end of the building, he was shown into a bare partitioned room where there were two other similarly dressed officials; one of them had some red braid on the shoulder.

David's companion said something to 'red braid' in Romanian and the only words that David recognised were 'Harry Robson'. Following this, one of the officials left the room, leaving David standing whilst the remaining officials continued talking in Romanian. Putting his bag down, David looked for a seat but there was none except that used by 'red braid'.

After about five minutes, the official returned and reported back to what was obviously the senior official. At the end of the report 'red braid' looked up.

"There is no Mr Harry Robson in Romania. Why are you making up this name?"

"I am not making up the name. Harry Robson comes to Romania regularly and was supposed to be here to meet me."

There were further exchanges between 'red braid' and the other official who turned to David.

"You will come with me." Again the hand was on the revolver. David went to pick up his bag. "And you will leave this here."

He was led away up the corridor and waved into another room that was bare but for a small table and one chair. Completely nonplussed, he sank on to the chair. This was not the exciting time he had foreseen.

So that was what took so long at the customs. The customs officer was looking at a list of people's names. They must have a ready access to information on who has entered Romania.

After a long period, the door opened and the official again appeared, beckoning David to come out and accompany him back to the original office, where he was again presented to 'red braid'.

"Mr Robson was here but he is not here now. Why do you say he is waiting for you? And why do you not know why you are here?"

"But I have already told your colleague why I am here. To visit some of your companies."

"Which companies?"

This was getting beyond a joke.

"Mr Robson has our itinerary. Perhaps he is arriving later today or tomorrow. Until he arrives I cannot answer your questions." David was wondering how he could possibly get out of this, when suddenly there was a nod from 'red braid'

"You have a hotel reservation?"

"Yes at the Theodore."

"You will go straight there and not wait any longer at the airport. You will book your taxi at the taxi desk."

With that, the first official indicated that he should pick up his bag and accompany him out of the office. Once in the main area, he was directed to a man sitting at a desk in the corner of the building.

"Theodore? That is 100 Lei." Four pounds! David thought that it seemed a lot of money but later learnt that because the taxis were run by the state it was the norm.

"Taxi number 56. You will find it outside."

Outside there were a number of cars, all of which he recognised were the Renault Dauphins that used to be popular in the England in the late1960s. On the top of each one was the taxi sign and a number. Most of them had their engines running and David was conscious of the pungent smell of the exhaust fumes. At the front was taxi number 56, which he approached. The driver immediately got out and, without a word, almost snatched the piece of brownish paper from him and proceeded to load the bags into the taxi.

During the twenty-minutes journey David reflected on how long it had taken him to get to Bucharest. He'd left Dagenham at 7.30 in the evening on Saturday and here he was, 5.30 p.m. on the Monday. After his rough reception, he was looking forward to being able to relax in his own hotel room. Looking out of the taxi window, he noticed that shortly after they left the countryside around the airport they were coming into a built-up area.

What struck him most was the lack of traffic. There was only a bus or two, and then other taxis. It felt strange after years driving on the crowded North Circular road around London. Finally, they arrived at the front of an ornate building with the large sign 'Theodore' half-way up the building.

The taxi driver unloaded the taxi and carried his bag through the entrance door, pulling aside the heavy curtain that hung just inside. David retained possession of his brief case and the driver led him to the reception desk. The interior looked pre-war, not unlike the Russell Hotel in London, but instead of marble there was an abundance of dark panelling and bedraggled aspidistras. The air was smoky and, under the cold florescent lights, it swirled as the outside door was opened. Approaching the reception desk, David felt relief that he had finally made it. The receptionist looked up. "Yes sir?"

"David Edwards," he announced. "I have a reservation from yesterday but you received a telex from me from Zurich airport telling you that I would be a little late." The receptionist looked down at some papers.

"I'm sorry sir but your room has been let. We let it go when you didn't arrive on Sunday." She said it in a matter of fact voice.

"But you had a telex, in fact you had two telexes. Look here are the copies."

The receptionist looked at the two pieces of paper, returned them, and proceeded in the same flat voice to say that they had not received them. This was impossible because the transmitting telex machine could only produce copies after it received acknowledgement that the transmission had been successful.

"It may have been received by our tourist office but it has not been received by us at the Theodore."

"But it was sent to the Theodore Hotel. I have the telex number here," David protested. "Sir, we are part of the Romanian State Tourist Board and our instructions come from them. You should go to the Romanian State Tourist office across the road and see if they can find you other accommodation." And with that the receptionist started to turn away.

It was time to locate Harry to see if he could sort something out. However, when he asked the receptionist if she could locate Harry, she replied, " Mr Robson is registered here but he has not yet booked in. His room is reserved because it was prepaid."

At that moment David felt very dejected. After all the problems he had had with the flight, the last thing that he wanted was problems with the accommodation.

Picking up his bag, he again pulled back the curtain protecting the swing doors from the chill November air and crossed the main street to an office that had a Romanian State Tourist sign over it. Inside there were a number of desks, each had a girl seated at it. Not knowing which desk he should approach, he stood for a while waiting for someone to enquire as to his business. Nothing happened.

Not one of the girls looked up.

Taking the bull by the horns, he strode up to the desk on the right and stood directly in front of the dark-haired girl sitting there. Still no movement.

"Excuse me."

"Yes?" said the girl slowly looking up. " I understand that you received a telex that was sent to the Theodore Hotel from Zurich." He showed her the copies. Rather disinterestedly she replied after giving them only a cursory glance. " We have never received them."

"But you must have," David insisted, "these are copies of the message transmitted." She shrugged her shoulders, "So what is your problem?"

" My problem? My problem is that my company reserved a room at the Theodore and I have been informed that there is no room at the Theodore or any other hotel."

Once he had taken this firm stand he wondered whether he really should have raised his voice like that, but it seemed to have an effect. The girl looked a little subdued and proceeded to dial a number on the telephone on her desk.

After a few minutes of talking, during which David sensed that there was some disagreement with the person at the other end, she put the telephone down and looked up. "You must go back to the Theodore. They have a room for you." With that she looked down leaving him standing totally confused.

Nothing more could be gained until he had once again visited the receptions desk at the Theodore. Crossing the main street, which was almost empty of traffic with the exception of some old battered buses and a few taxis, he once more pushed through the heavy curtain, negotiating his bags through the swing doors into the reception area. The smoky atmosphere appeared even more acrid. Approaching the same receptionist who has previously denied knowledge of the telex, David attracted her attention by stating: "I understand that you do have a room for me."

" Ah, Mr Edwards. Yes, we have found a room or rather a suite. It is our penthouse suite. It is on the sixth floor. There is of course a surcharge on your voucher. It will be fifteen US dollars per day extra. Please can you pass over the voucher so that we can alter it? We will keep this and return it when you leave, marked up with the extra charged to your travel agent. Your passport please. This you can have back tomorrow. Here is the key to the sixth floor suite."

It was all a little too much, but he didn't have the energy to argue. It was now getting on for 7 o'clock and he was feeling very weary. No one stepped forward to help him with his bags. He looked round and saw the lift doors. First pressing the up button then once inside pressing the '6' button, the lift started, first slowly then a little faster. When it stopped the doors opened on to a corridor. Opposite was a door marked 'P'. He tried the key and found that the door opened.

The suite, which consisted of a sitting area and bedroom area, was furnished in the same 1920s style as that of the foyer, with heavy oak-panelled wardrobes, an old coloured lamp standard and puce coloured green and cream décor. A heavy duvet covered the bed, a bulbous heavy moquette covered settee and armchair stood in the sitting area. The lights had square cornered shades, typical of the fashion at that time. One could almost imagine a Charleston girl, complete with cigarette holder, popping out of the similarly furnished bathroom. If only…. At least he had a bed.

Not feeling the least bit hungry, he decided that he would open up the half bottle of whisky that he'd managed to retain and pour himself a stiff tot. After that, he proceeded to pack away some of his clothes in the deep drawers of the chest of drawers, leaving out his pyjamas and dressing gown. He might as well use the sitting accommodation he thought and while he was about it, why not have another nip of the malt? He'd read only about five pages of Neville Shute's *A Town like Alice* when his eyelids started to become heavy.

It may be the Scotch, he thought, and decided that he would do the rest of the reading in bed. He woke up some one hour later to find the book loosely clutched in his right hand and the reading light still on. He put the book to one side, set his alarm clock to 7 o'clock and turned the light out, falling into a deep sleep within seconds.

Chapter 4

At first he couldn't quite orientate himself. There was a loud ringing. Realising that it was his alarm clock, he reached out and pressed the brass knob on the top. As he slowly remembered where he was, he wondered how he was going to manage without Harry Robson. At least he had to start doing something so, rolling down from the high bed, he made his way to the antiquated bathroom and started to run a bath. After some spluttering from the hot-water tap, the bath started to fill with acceptably hot water.

Whilst the bath filled, he shaved with his cordless electric razor, finishing just in time to step into the now full bath. It relaxed him a little, but the anxiety of his situation caused him to hurry through his ablutions and dry himself quickly. He began to dress, putting on clean underwear and selected a smart shirt and tie; he was just tackling his tie when the telephone rang.

"Hello. Is that David? Harry here, Harry Robson. Sorry I wasn't here when you arrived. I understand you had a bit of bother with the room." A bit of bother with the room! "Anyway when you're ready I'll meet you in the restaurant for what they call breakfast." With that he rang off. David wondered how would he know Harry Robson. Perhaps he'll make a sign or something, he thought, and with that he hurriedly slipped on his suit jacket, picked up the room key, and left the room leaving his pyjamas thrown on the bed and the room generally untidy.

True enough, as he entered the dining room his attention was attracted by the waving of a hand that belonged to a pleasant-looking man who was also dressed in a suit. "David. Over here." It was comforting to feel the warm welcome, the square shaped face breaking into a smile. On looking closer, he readjusted his estimate of Harry's age. Premature baldness made him look older, perhaps in his late thirties or early forties at the most. He was about David's height and he carried a few too many pounds but otherwise he was the typical Englishman.

"Sit yerself down. Coffee? I've got Turkish but you can have Nescafé if you want." David looked at the small black cup in front of Harry and elected for the latter. "I'm afraid that you will only get rather stale bread and jam but it will keep you going." He waved to one of the waiters who after a number of waves decided to come across and take the order. "I understand that you had some problems on the way."

David related his experiences. When he came to the room fiasco Harry's brows closed. "The bastards have taken you for more dollars." He explained that he was quite sure that the original room booked was still available and that the whole charade was designed and executed to get a higher hotel charge out of him. "Still there was nothing you could do. The principals get the bill anyway and, divided by two, it won't cause too much of a ripple."

"Now, first, welcome to K.M. and Romania. As Peter Osbourne probably said, Romania is not as easy as Hungary." He hadn't, but never mind. "There are certain rules that you have to observe, but I'll take you through them as we go along. Our programme is that we will be in Romania for the rest of the week, it doesn't matter that we've lost a day. All that will happen is that the Enterprises will keep us stewing for the contracts one day less. Then, on Saturday, we motor through to Budapest for our second week. You will be going back after that and I will carry on to Yugoslavia."

The waiter arrived with a cup of black coffee and a plate of thick grey looking slices of bread, a big knob of butter and some rather thick jam.

"Get stuck in, but don't rush. Our first meeting is not until 10 o'clock."

"I don't know anything about the programme," David apologised, wondering if Harry thought he had been briefed more than he had.

"I'll let you have a full copy when we are on our way. Our first meeting is with Romconstructimpex. This is the Enterprise that deals with all new buildings and restructuring of buildings and plant. Wait. You do know the set-up with regard to Enterprises?" When David admitted that he didn't, Harry's brows came down again. "Peter should have briefed you on that at least."

Harry then went on to explain that under the State-run system in Romania, all buying and selling was carried out by Enterprises, each of which usually represented a whole industry. He explained that they would be visiting two on this trip: Romconstructimpex and Romchemimpex. The former, as already explained, covered the requirements for the construction industry and the latter covered all the buying and selling of chemical and ancillary products.

"Although the people in general in Romania are very pleasant, those connected with business are all bastards. They have to be, otherwise they're in trouble with the Communist member overseeing them." It sounded like Reds under the bed! "We will be dealing with up to three members of the Enterprise when we discuss our quotation and they must win adjustments to the original offer or they suffer humiliation or even worse. Hence we play the game. Today, when we visit Romconstructimpex we will be told that our offer is totally unacceptable and we will present some resistance to changing it. After perhaps an hour and a half we will agree to re-think our prices. Then tonight I will send a telex to Peter, back home, explaining the difficulty. He will come back with the authority for us to make a slightly lower offer by reducing our prices by a further 5%. Romconstructimpex will possibly know of this before we do."

"I don't understand," David interjected. "How can they know about what is sent to you here at the hotel?"

"Because when the telex is received a copy will be passed to both of the Enterprises that we are visiting." He paused and then realised. "Of course, you couldn't tell them who we were visiting when you booked in because you didn't know then. That is why I had to give them the information when I booked in."

"I just said that I was visiting customers with you."

"It is a condition of your reservation," Harry continued, "that you disclose who you are visiting during your stay at the hotel. The hotel then passes on any information that may be helpful to the Enterprises possibly at the same time or even before you receive it."

David was beginning to feel a distinctly uneasy over so much commercial intrigue.

"The fact that you are visiting with me covered you. They already have my information."

"But what happens when we present the new prices?"

"They will receive them without, obviously, letting on that they knew of them." Harry paused again.

"And then what?"

"They'll reject them again."

"But that's ridiculous," said David, "what do they hope to gain by this charade?"

"Even better prices," smiled Harry. "We will insist that there can be no further reductions and they will insist that we have another meeting. We will reluctantly agree and, when we meet up, I will pretend to be totally dejected and concede a further 3%, suggesting that they probably won't see me again because I am likely to get fired when I return home. Then we sign the contract."

"But what about when you get back?" asked David now, very perturbed.

"What do you mean?" questioned Harry calmly.

"Well, taking it upon yourself to reduce the prices." That was something that David had never been allowed to do at Arkus without Reg Wilson's OK.

"Sorry David. I should have mentioned that the final final price, that is the so-called final reduction, has already been agreed with Priory Paints. It's their quotation. You see, we need to provide a way in which the negotiators can keep the Communist members happy and their noses clean."

"But surely your contacts must know that this is a bit of a game?"

"Of course, but the game must be played. It's the only way to do business in Romania. It's a little easier in Hungary, and Yugoslavia is almost a capitalist country under Tito anyway."

David's head was spinning but, before he could try to make sense of this, Harry indicated that they should set off for their first meeting. They would take a taxi to the office of Romconstructimpex as it would take too long to get a release ticket out of the underground garage for his 1800, the company car that he used in Eastern Europe. Anyway, the offices were only a few blocks away in Boulevard Diniscu Golescu.

The taxi was booked and paid for at the reception; apparently you never paid the driver as all taxis were run by the State Tourist Agency. Harry gave the address of Romconstructimpex and the two of them settled in the back of the Dacia. These were Renaults assembled in Romania under licence. There were very few cars on the road, but there were some quite antiquated buses running along the Boulevard Mageheru, the street outside the Hotel. David made a note of the name of the street in case he got lost. The buses seemed to emit more exhaust than those in London and the smell was distinctly acrid. Then he saw a 'bendy bus', a bus joined in the middle with a concertina cover. It was all very different from back home.

They arrived at the Romconstructimpex offices. The building was rather ornate in style and obviously quite old. It reminded David of the Albert Hall in London; with red brick façade and ornate moulding half way up the facade. They passed through a gateway in the railings and a short drive led to the front of the building. Alighting from the taxi, they found themselves at the foot of some stone steps that led up to a large high entrance with double doors. To David's surprise, the doors opened outwards and a wall of heavy blanket confronted them.

"'It gets bloody cold here in the winter." Harry saw my expression. "It helps to keep the warmth in."

Once beyond the blanket, there was a fog of cigarette smoke. From the smell, David could now believe the story that cigarettes were made out of ground rubber. Like the hotel, the entrance was in the 1920's style, even down to an aspidistra in the corner. Harry approached the reception window. David thought that the receptionist deliberately put her head down as they approached, keeping them waiting a full three or four minutes before she looked up. In spite of this, Harry gave her a broad smile.

"Good morning. How are you?" There wasn't any reply. "We have an appointment with Mr Alexandru." She took his card and disappeared.

"When you get into the interview room, offer your cigarettes to Mr Alexandru and his assistant Mrs Fiore. They'll each take one. Then push the whole twenty pack towards Mr Alexandru. He will say 'Thank you', then put the packet in his pocket."

"Does he always do that?"

"Of course. They really go for Western cigarettes, understandable after the taste of the local brands. Hold on here we go."

A rather stately women, about 40 years old, had appeared at the door and was coming over to them. "Madam Fiore. How nice to see you again." Then, to David's absolute amazement, Harry took her hand and raised to it to his lips. 'I could really never do that,' thought David. 'I think I would rather die than have to do that.'

The woman accepted the gesture with a smile and returned Harry's greeting. Harry turned and nodded towards me. "This is my colleague who will be looking after you in the future – David Edwards. David – Mrs Fiore."

"How do you do." Mrs Fiore spoke with only a slight accent, bowing her head a little. "Er. How do you do." David replied.

"Mr Alexandru is waiting for us in the interview room." Madame Fiore led the way up a wide shallow-stepped balustrade staircase. David almost felt that if everything were in black and white it would look just like a 1920's film set. At the top of the staircase they followed Mrs Fiore along a passageway. Finally they turned into a room on the right, entering through very tall double doors. At one end David observed a plastic-topped table behind which sat a Latin looking man, similar in looks to the man that he had seen breakfasting at the Aerial hotel.

"Hallo Mr Alexandru. It's very nice to see you again." "And you," came the reply, "I trust that you had a good journey?"

"Well, I did. But my colleague David Edwards had some problems with the flights and the hotel booking. David, may I introduce you to Mr Alexandru – Enterprise buyer for surface treatment materials. Mr Alexandru – David Edwards who will be looking after you in the future." David grasped the outstretched hand and was surprised how firm it was. He had expected a limp handshake. He didn't know why, it just went with the furnishings.

"Welcome to Romania, Mr Edwards. I hope that you enjoy your stay here. Now let me see, Edwards. Is that a Welsh name?" "No," David replied, explaining that he came from London. That was easier than explaining Dagenham in Essex.

"Ah then you wouldn't be a JPR fan then?" What the hell was he talking about? Then came a nudge from Harry and a whisper. "Rugby, J. P. R. Williams."

"Oh the famous JPR." David managed to recover his composure, remembering that Romania had a strong international Rugby team. "You don't have to be Welsh to recognise that talent. But we do beat the Welsh from time to time." He was struggling. West Ham, ' the 'ammers', the East London soccer team, was more his cup of tea.

"We haven't yet had that honour but it may come one day." The preliminaries over, they all sat down.

"When are you going back?" It was just as Harry had said. They ask you this so that they know how long they can prolong the bargaining before you have to leave.

"Friday, but I'm sure that we can complete our business and celebrate the contract with a good lunch together before then."

"I am not so sure," said Mr Alexandru; Madame Fiore sat in silence. "We were very disappointed with your quotation. I am afraid that we cannot do business at these prices."

David thought that he saw a little nod from Harry and remembered the cigarette act. Pulling out a packet of Piccadilly, he offered the packet to Madame Fiore and then to Mr Alexandru. Both smiled and accepted. Harry drew out a lighter and the smell of smoke – this time not quite so unacceptable- started to fill the room, David pushed the packet towards Mr Alexandru. He smiled and, almost like an actor in a Noel Coward play, closed the packet and slid it into his pocket.

"Mr Alexandru, then you have already received our quotation for the Priory Paints heat resisting grade paint?"

"Yes." Mr Alexandu's expression had changed. "We were very disappointed with the prices."

"Mr Alexandru," it was Harry's turn to change expression, "those prices are very competitive. I would be very surprised if you could get a better offer anywhere."

"But Mr Robson. Why are they 12% higher than last year?" Now the battle was underway. David felt as if he were sitting in the theatre stalls with a performance just about to begin.

"In fact they are lower than our national inflation which is running at about 15% at the present time."

"Inflation?" a little of the warmth had gone out of Mr Alexandru's voice. "What is all this about inflation?" Mrs Fiore continued to sit silently without any change in expression or participation in the exchanges.

"Mr Alexandru," Harry had firmed up his tone a little, "when I came to see you earlier this year I paid 25 Lei for the taxi from the Theodore. Today they charged me 30 Lei. That's a lot more that 12%. More like 20%. So you have inflation here as well."

A little pause, and then deciding not to respond to that, Mr Alexandru tried a different tack. "The quantities should have helped keep the price pegged at the same as last year, which is what we are looking for."

"Mr Alexandru, although I will most likely be severely criticised, if we can finalise the contract now, I will tell our people that we could negotiate only at £2.13p per kilo because of the increased quantities. That is a 5% reduction." Harry looked expectantly at his negotiating counterpart.

"But Mr Robson we cannot agree any price increase."

"I am sorry, Mr Alexandru but there is no way that we can hold last year's prices, so perhaps we will have to miss out on this occasion." Wow! What was he doing? David thought he'd had a sheltered life up to now. This was adrenaline-raising stuff. Even at his age he could feel a quickening of his heart rate.

"I am sure that your Mr Osbourne will be able to help us find a solution." The smile was back.

"I'll pass on your concerns, but there is hardly enough profit in the prices for us to be able to make adjustments."

"We will be available on Thursday at the same time." Mrs Fiore still hadn't said a word, but she now rose from her chair to indicate that the meeting was over.

After a few more general pleasantries they took their leave. The cigarette smoke in the entrance hall appeared even thicker now than when they had gone in, but they had to endure it for only a short time before they pushed their way through the blanket and out into the open air again.

"That's a blow," said David, when they were out in the street again. "Does that mean that we won't get the order?"

"Of course we'll get the order."

"But—."

"As I said," interrupted Harry, "it's par for the course to reject the first offer. When we make the final final offer they will sign the contract."

"The final final?" This was all Romania speak to David. "Yes. We offer the next lowest price and then concede the price we really want, very reluctantly, to close the deal."

Once outside the railings, they turned right and walked along Boulevard Diniscu Golescu. David wasn't sure why, but he didn't like to question Harry about it at that moment.

"But what about Madam Fiore? Why didn't she take part in the discussion?"

"Because she was only there as the Party member."

"Party member?"

"Yes she reports back to the Director on what Alexandru said. It's part of the control system, David." There was a small trace of irritation in his voice now. "This is Communism. It doesn't work like the West."

Then perhaps realising that his tone might have sounded harsh, he smiled. "It takes a bit of getting used to but you'll soon get the hang of things."

David thought that it was time to find out what was going to happen next.

"Are we going to Romchemimpex now?"

"Yes, They're only in Calea Grivitei – about a ten minute walk from here."

They walked on in silence for some time. Then Harry began to explain the background to Romchemimpex.

Suddenly, Harry stopped and touched David's arm. "Let's cross over." His voice sounded rather urgent. They crossed over to an empty side street and continued to walk on. Harry was silent for a minute. Thinking that he had said something wrong, David questioned why they had needed to cross the road.

"Don't worry, it's nothing." Then perhaps feeling that a more detailed explanation was required, after a pause, Harry went on.

"You perhaps didn't see the man about 30 yards in front? Well, from his manner I feel sure that he would have accosted us as we passed."

"What attacked two us?"

"No, offered us black market money."

David remembered what his companion on the plane had said; the man could be a police informer or even part of the police force. It seemed almost too weird to be true.

"It has happened before when I had just turned down a demand to adjust the price. Luckily there were no repercussions, but the police did stop and search me, which was worrying and time wasting."

David was just able to see the man as they turned the corner into the main street. Harry went on explaining the background to Romachemimpex almost as if nothing had happened. Apparently the company was the part of the Enterprise for the processing industries, which had taken it over only last year. Up to then, Romgummimpex had been a separate import and export Enterprise for the rubber manufacturing industry. Romgummimpex was now combined with Romchemimpex, which now served the whole plastics, rubber and dyeing industries

The two of them arrived at the offices of Romchemimpex. These were in a similar Victorian type building to those of Romconstructimpex with ornate brickwork and fussy iron railings just outside the entrance. This time there was no blanket shielding the front door but the interior was similarly smogged with tobacco smoke. The wooden-panelled walls were tinged with yellow from the nicotine of the dense tobacco smoke. What they put in the cigarettes David could not imagine.

Harry approached the reception window, waited while the girl inside finished her conversation with her companion, then he presented his card and announced that they had come to visit Mr Ilescu.

The receptionist, who, up to this point hadn't said a word, picked up the cream and grey telephone and conveyed what he guessed was an announcement of their arrival. It was a pity that she didn't smile because she was actually quite attractive, with a neat figure, maybe a little broad across the beam, a delicate pear shaped face and dark shiny hair.

His mind was beginning to generate a few fantasies when another young lady appeared. Unlike the receptionist, she had a smile on her face and, with her fair hair, projected a more sparkling personality.

"Mr Robson," her eyes then flashed towards David. David's fantasies changed only by the hair colour and more intimate thoughts came to mind. He was jolted out of his reveries when Harry spoke.

"Hello Matti, as lovely as ever," to which her smile became even broader and a slight blush came to her cheeks. This deepened when Harry raised her offered hand to his lips. Letting go of her hand, he turned to David.

"And this is Mr Edwards." David took the outstretched hand. "Welcome to Romania, Mr Edwards. Mr Robson has told us that you would be accompanying him." Then, turning to Harry, "Mr Ilescu is ready for you."

True to form, as he now knew, there was a 'party member' present with Mr Ilescu. "You remember Mr Coman, Mr Robson?" "Of course." Harry shook hands with Mr Coman then perhaps a little more warmly with Mr Ilescu, who greeted him with a little more warmth than had Mr Alexandru at our previous meeting.

It then became clear where Matti fitted in. She was the interpreter. Mr Ilescu spoke in Romanian, which was then translated by Matti, but David had the impression that Mr Ilescu understood Harry's English. After a few more pleasantries, with Mr Ilescu showing sympathy for David's travel and accommodation difficulties, the negotiations followed the same pattern as before. The charade was played out and a further meeting was arranged for the following Thursday.

David felt that he was beginning to get the feel of things, although he still could not get used to the smoke haze in the buildings. This was only equalled by the sour smell of the exhaust fumes from the buses in the streets. Matti had arranged for a taxi to be called and it was not long before they arrived back in the Theodore Hotel.

"Matti seems nice," David ventured while they were taking a beer on the terrace.

"Very nice, but if you are getting ideas forget them. The Romanians are not allowed to fraternise with Westerners except through business. It's even stricter than that. If they do have contact, by accident of course, they have to report their conversation to the police within 24 hours."

"But what about the blokes I saw in the lift when I went up to my room last night? They seemed to be doing all right."

"They're the idiots who don't know the ropes. The birds they've pulled are actually State prostitutes. When they go into their negotiations, if they're in sales, they will be reminded of their indiscretion and pressurised by a veiled threat to send details of their exploits back home."

David sat quietly, listening in near disbelief. It must be true: there was no reason to lie.

Harry had changed the subject, "After we've had lunch, we'll go to the Embassy Club and have a few beers."

He explained over lunch – at least that's what he called the meal that they ate at 4.30 in the afternoon – that the British Embassy ran a club to protect Westerners from the attention of fake black market money changers offering attractive rates of exchange, and from the State prostitutes. The Club provided any Western visitors with a picture show on Thursday and Friday evenings, and cards and dominoes with cheap beer on the other nights.

Following Harry's advice, David chose the pork cutlet. "Pork's the usual meat in Eastern Europe. Beef's a bit dodgy; you don't know how long it's been around. Chips are always greasy but you'll soon get used to them."

They arranged to meet at 7 o'clock and David returned to his room, he read his Neville Shute paperback. After some time he tired of reading and went out on to his balcony to watch the street below. Even from that height he could smell the exhaust fumes of the buses. As he looked down on an articulated bus that had seen better days, he began to wonder where the Romanians bought them.

He could see the department store on the other side of the street, but he had been advised that, except for large piles of boots, which had been delivered from the State-owned shoe factory that week, there was little else to purchase.

At 7 o'clock David went down to the foyer to meet Harry and they set off for the Embassy Club, only a few minutes walk away in the street Jules Michelet. The Embassy building stood in its own grounds and had a khaki-uniformed guard at the entrance. Harry led David to the side building that served as the Club for Western visitors.

As soon as he entered he could feel the British atmosphere. A man in a blazer, a little older than David, came forward to greet them, giving Harry a warm welcome.

"Hello Harry, back to the grind again?"

"Not for too long now. George, I'd like you to meet David Edwards, my replacement here in Romania. David has just joined K.M. and is here learning the ropes. Perhaps I'll accompany him on a few more trips, but he's officially taking over the territory from me on this visit. David — George Fox, First Commercial Secretary."

"Welcome to Romania, David," the hand outstretched again. "Make this your second home when you come to Bucharest. The Embassy Club is not only a pleasant place to come to, at least we think it is, but it'll keep you out of mischief."

Harry wandered off to talk to a person wearing a similar blazer and cravat to George, the First Commercial Secretary. As soon as he was out of earshot, David confided to George.

"Harry has been putting me right on things to look out for, but I must admit it all sounds a bit dramatic."

"Believe all he tells you." George suddenly became more serious. "Romania is perhaps more Communist than Russia. Certainly Ceauşescu rules it with a firmer iron fist. Basically the Romanians are very nice people – you'll find that out if you visit the country where the party members are thinner on the ground. However, here in Bucharest, they are controlled to such an extent that they would shop their own grandmother if they had to." Smiling again he took David by the elbow, "Come let me buy the first beer." He led him to the bar where a white-coated barman pulled off the cap of a beer bottle and handed him a glass.

"All drinks are 2 Lei, that's just over 1.6d in old money to you. Oh, by the way, let me introduce you to Siegfried Muller, Siggie as he likes to be called. He can tell you a thing or two. He travels the whole of Eastern Europe and parts of Asia buying sausage skins. "Siggie," he called out to a small rounded chap of about forty.

"Siggie, I'd like you to meet David. It's his first visit to Bucharest.'

"Hi." Although the expression was American, Siggie had a slightly guttural tone.

"You've come to the right place for a bit of relaxation, anyway."

"I came with Harry. I'm taking over his area for K.M."

"Great guy, Harry," replied Siggie. Now David could place the accent; it was German. "We've sunk a few together, but unfortunately they don't stock Geneva here." David was to learn later that Siggie could put away quite a few drinks in an evening and his preference was Dutch Geneva gin, which was sold only at the Intercontinental Hotel.

"George tells me you are in sausage skins." It seemed a ridiculous thing to say, but at that moment David couldn't think of any other way of putting it.

"That's right. I expect you find that a little unusual; most people do."

"I'd never thought about it," replied David rather taken aback by the blunt approach. "In fact, if you'd asked me where sausage skins came from I couldn't have told you. Is Romania a good place for them?"

"Yes," replied Siggie. "Though not as good as Mongolia."

"You go there too?" He'd rather warmed to the subject now.

"Yes. And I can tell you that whatever you think about Romanian food, Mongolian food is ten times worse. But the sausage skins are good. You see the sheep and goats scratch around for fodder and have to be tough."

"Do you come here often?" How many times had he used that phrase as chat up line on the dance floor? However, this time he was interested in the answer.

"About once every two months."

"How do you find it?"

"Not too bad. You see, I'm buying. I'm in a different position from you. The Romanians don't have to try to compromise me, which means that where you can only look, I can touch as well. Getting close to the Romanian beauties makes life in Romania bearable." David could well believe that, remembering Matti.

"Is it really as dangerous as Harry has told me? The black market money vendors and the prostitutes?"

"You'd better believe it, David. If you're here to negotiate a contract, they'll do anything to put you at a disadvantage. It's a bit different when you get out of Bucharest, especially in the smaller villages. But even there, there is likely to be a party member." Harry drifted back to join them.

"David, there is a show on at the Intercontinental. You might enjoy it, would you like to go? It begins about 10 o'clock and lasts for about an hour, so you won't lose too much shuteye. Interested?"

"It's worth seeing," prompted Siggie.

"In that case, yes, of course," said David.

At that point they were joined by George Fox. "Incidentally, there's a rumble on the grape vine that there's some trouble 'at t' mill' in the Ministry of Industry. Don't know the details yet, but Dobraescu, that's our Romania clerk, was overheard saying something to one of the Romanian cleaners. He doesn't know that there are one or two people in the Embassy who understand Romanian. We don't let the locals know who can speak their language; it comes in quite useful at times."

"What sort of trouble?" enquired Harry.

"'Not clear yet, but we'll keep you posted."

A little later Harry indicated that it was time they should go. They walked the few blocks to the Intercontinental, which stood on the corner at the end of Boulevard Bălcescu. The hotel was only recently built, and was very American in style and decor. Harry made for the lift, entered and pressed the button marked 'Restaurant'. The lift rose, but stopped on the fifth floor where a red-faced American accompanied by a brassy Romanian blonde got in.

Harry looked sidewise at David, who didn't register the meaning of the look. Later Harry explained that the blonde was one of the State prostitutes, adding that the American would regret the pleasure and would pay for it later. David knew what he meant now. Having reached the top floor, Harry and David arrived at the restaurant, which apparently also served as a cabaret room.

They found a table fairly near the edge of the dance floor that was already occupied by one person, who they learned was a fellow countryman named Trevor. Harry ordered some drinks, which cost him four times as much as downstairs in the bar. They sat watching a few couples dancing for about 15 minutes. The red-faced American was among them. Suddenly the light dimmed and an announcement, first in German then in English, heralded the State Theatre dancers.

They were followed by Romanian music from the small orchestra in the corner of the dance floor and the entrance, from the side of the orchestra, of brightly-dressed Romanian dancers. David assumed that they were in National costume; something Harry confirmed a few minutes later. From the colour and design of the costumes, he could understand why his flight companion bought Romanian country clothing. David could imagine that it would have a ready market in the West.

The dancing was well performed and generated generous applause. It was followed by another, more vigorous routine and then a third dance that came to a frenzied crescendo. The dancers gave a bow and danced their way off the floor, leaving only the faint whiff of body odour. The orchestra played a few more orchestral Romanian pieces, followed by a male soloist singing Romanian ballads.

When the orchestra started to pack away their instruments, the sudden quietness allowed David and Harry to talk to Trevor who, they learned, worked for the UK arm of the General Electric and Power Generating Corporation. Apparently he was a commissioning engineer and was putting in a generating station for the Romanian Government. He had been in Bucharest for about two months. Now he was finding life a little lonely following the dispatch home of his colleague two weeks before to deal with another contract somewhere in the Far East. Trevor was staying at the Theodore Hotel and readily agreed to walk back with David and Harry and join them for a night-cap in the hotel bar.

After just two drinks they all retired for the night, agreeing to meet the next morning at breakfast at 9 o'clock.

Chapter 5

Waking a little early, David decided to go down and get some fresh air before meeting up with Harry as arranged. On passing the reception desk, he noticed Trevor, in a very agitated state, having a heated exchange with the desk clerk. David stood back a polite distance but was noticed by Trevor when he turned away from the desk.

"Anything wrong?" asked David.

"Too bloody right there is," replied Trevor, still obviously very upset.

"I have just been told that my room is no longer available. No reason, just that it isn't available."

"What do you mean 'No longer available'?"

"Just that." Trevor was no longer the quiet introvert that they had spent the previous evening with.

"But surely they gave you a reason?"

"That's the most frustrating part about it. They just kept repeating that it wasn't available."

"What are you going to do?"

"They said that if I go to the State Tourist office across the road, they will find me private accommodation outside of Bucharest." David recalled his experience with that office when he arrived.

"Is that bad?"

"From what I have heard, private accommodation can be very primitive and fleas are not unknown is some of the country areas."

"What are you going to do?" David felt helpless.

"Get the first bloody plane out. As far as I am concerned they can build their generating station themselves." Still very upset, Trevor was already striding towards the Tarom airline representative who had a table in the large foyer. Unable to be of any help, David made his way to the breakfast area where he was relieved to see Harry was already seated. He related what had happened to Trevor; Harry looked perturbed.

"There must be a logical reason for it, but to winkle it from these devious bastards, is not easy.... Trevor!" He'd seen Trevor enter the breakfast room and beckoned him over.

"Any luck with the flight?"

"He is going to come back to me."

"That means that he is going to report your request to the Ministry. I wouldn't expect any immediate action if I were you. Look we're driving to our meeting at 11 o'clock. Why don't we give you a lift to Otopeni Airport where you could try the SwissAir desk yourself?"

"That's very kind of you. I might take you up on that."

Whilst they had been talking, coffee, hot water and Nescafe packets had arrived for the three of them, together with some stale rolls and some unsalted butter and jam. Trevor started to eat, engrossed by his own thoughts. Harry and David also ate in silence. Just as they were about to leave, a young Romanian appeared in the door of the breakfast room and hurried over to Trevor. After whispering something in his ear, he withdrew to the far corner of the room.

"That's my interpreter, Dominique." Trevor explained. "Will you excuse me for a moment." He got up and joined the young man in the corner. After about five minutes he returned. His expression was even grimmer than before.

"How stupid can they get? You were right Harry. The Tarom rep moved fast and Dominique was told to hurry over to correct things." Harry and David waited for the story to unfold.

"It appears," Trevor continued, "that for some stupid reason they think that I am stretching out the work so that I can spend more time in Bucharest. Can you believe it? As if anyone in their right mind would want to spend longer than they have to here. 'First prize is one week in Bucharest, second prize is two weeks in Bucharest'."

"I'm still not with you." David said.

"Because they think that I want to stay here, they decided to make it 'less comfortable' for me. Hence the withdrawal of accommodation at the marvellous Theodore." Trevor's attitude had now changed to one of indignation. "Apparently, when the light flashed that it wasn't going to work and finding out that I intended to leave, my room inexplicably became available again."

"What do you intend to do? Take up the room again?" Harry was still concerned.

"Not on your Nellie. As far as I am concerned they can finish the works themselves. I'll take up your suggestion and try to book the SwissAir flight direct. But I won't take up your offer for a lift because, if when I phone there is a flight today, and I think that there is, I'll pack my bags and take a taxi straight out to the Airport. At any rate I know that there is one tomorrow if today's is booked."

"Best of luck," called Harry, as Trevor hurriedly left the table, too preoccupied to reply.

"Phew, that's a turn up for the book," David commented.

"Nothing will surprise you when you've been here a few times," replied Harry." Anyway, down to business. We will be taking the car, so we need to leave a little time to get it out from the garage. We are going to The August 23 Works, which is a little way out of Bucharest."

"That's a strange name for a works."

"It's named after the 'liberation day' – the day that the Russians moved in at the end of the war," explained Harry. "There is an industrial department there and we need to meet up with the head of the Specification Department to get the details of the new construction project which hopefully could use Priory Paints." David left Harry to get the docket needed to get the Austin 1800 out of the underground garage and followed him into the lift down to the basement. He'd always liked the 1800 and understood that he would be able to pick up the one that had been ordered for him on his return to London. The Austin 1800 remained permanently in Romania, apparently, in the Eastern European territory for use on sales visits.

They set off, and David was relieved to see how empty the streets were of traffic. He would have no trouble driving in Romania. After about three quarters of an hour, they arrived at the works entrance gates, which were guarded by a khaki-uniformed soldier. No attempt was made to stop them and they drove through the gates and up to an office block at the end of the factory.

"Why the soldier?" queried David.

"There is no unemployment in Romania. Everyone is employed in some job or other. Therefore there are a lot of army personnel just to keep up employment numbers. They've got to find something to do with them." David remembered the large number of soldiers at Otopeni airport. Leaving the car, Harry and David entered the building whose reception was staffed by a further three people. After receiving their visitor's passes they were shown where they had to park the car. Returning to the entrance gate, they followed the uniformed gateman to a large old-fashioned block at the other end of the main building. It reminded David a little of the Priory Paints premises in London's Silvertown. Following the gateman up some stone steps, they passed through some large wooden doors and followed him along the corridor to another door at the end. They knocked and entered and were met by a big beaming man about 50 years old.

"Come in Mr Robson." The welcome seemed genuine. He then looked expectantly at me.

"David Edwards. He's just joined K.M. and will be taking over from me in due course. "David — Mr Dorobanti." (David later learned that that was how the name was spelled, but Harry did not pronounce the last 'i'.) "It is nice to see you Mr Dorobanti. You are still busy?"

"We keep going." It was the cautious response that Harry expected. "You've heard of the expected new project for the Boiler Plant then?"

"Yes. I was lucky enough to ask the right questions at the right time." Harry was equally non-committal.

"Well you are lucky," Mr Dorobanti commented. "It's got to be finished very quickly, so getting your quotation in early will give you a better chance of winning the contract. I don't think that the call for tenders has been officially announced yet."

Harry made no further comment and the two started to discuss the requirements. For the first time David was able to use some of the product information he had received from his visit at Priory Paints. At the end of the discussion, which lasted some hour and a half, various Priory Paints brand names 'or equivalents' had been written into the specification. Clever, thought David. He could learn a lot from Harry. Although Harry probed to find out about further future projects, he could not draw Dorobanti, who seemed to be reticent about giving out any information about future activities.

After a few more pleasantries, they bade their leave. The gateman was called and they were escorted back to their car.

"That was lucky that you heard of the Boiler plant project," David commented.

"You just have to keep your ears open and sometimes you get lucky."

They made their way to Bucharest, arriving back at the Hotel Theodore at about 2.30 p.m., just in time to have a snack in the dining room. David ordered an omelette – Harry advised him not to try the hamburger as it had upset his stomach last time that he had had it.

After they had eaten, Harry said that he would like to spend a little time in his room going through the specification he'd received so that he could put together the report for Priory Paints.

"Perhaps you'd like to come up and look over my shoulder, it could give you a bit of help in understanding how some of these go together."

"That would be great." He couldn't fault Harry. He'd been very helpful. David hoped that he could get up to an equal standard by the time he had to go it alone. There was an awful lot to learn. They worked on until about 5 p.m., by which time David had absorbed some of the information on the various paint products. He realised that he still had to get to grips with the product range and applications, but at least he now knew where to look up the required properties in the product manual.

"Right," said Harry, "the Embassy Club will be open in half an hour. We've earned a beer."

"You have," said David.

"Anyway lets have a quick shower and poodle round for one and sixpence worth. It was funny how Harry referred to old money.

They met in the reception area. Trevor was nowhere to be seen. Within a few minutes they passed the soldier guarding the entrance to the grounds of the embassy. Heading to the right of the main building, they entered the club building to find that some of the embassy staff were already there.

George, who he'd met on his first visit, was the first to greet them.

"The sun has gone down over the yardarm so it's all right to take an early beer. Had a good day Harry?"

"Not bad." There was a quick glance in David's direction, which David took as a 'keep your mouth shut' look.

"That's good. One needs a little good news from time to time. Today has been a bad one for us."

"Why, what's wrong?" David noticed that Harry was really concerned.

"They've shot Golescu."

"Paul Golescu?"

"Yes."

"The Minister for Construction?"

"Yes."

"There's been an assassination?" David felt he should make some contribution to the staccato conversation.

"No," said George "He's been executed. By a firing squad. He was found guilty of 'treason against the State' and shot this morning. Our Romanian admin chappie told us about it this morning. It's not fully out yet."

"What did he do to be found guilty of treason?" David couldn't believe that he was hearing this.

"Apparently he was passing information to a Westerner on proposed construction projects before they were generally announced."

"Is that so bad?" To David it was still beyond belief that someone could be shot for something so relatively trivial."

"It is a crime against the State."

"But how did they find out?" asked Harry who had gone slightly quiet.

"He was found to have some US dollars in his apartment. Harry explained to David that Romanians were not allowed to hold foreign money in Romania.

"Why is that bad for you George?" asked David.

"Because until they find out who the Westerner is, they will make life difficult for all of us, as well as all the embassy staff. There will be difficulties put in the way of everything we try to do. Meetings will be cancelled, visas will be delayed, oh and anything you can imagine. It almost makes us wish that they could find the silly bugger who's been slipping the late Minister a Dollar, Deutschmark, Schilling, Guilder or two. I can't believe it would be any of our lot. We know them all and none of them would be so daft as to get involved in this sort of thing."

"What will happen when they do find out the guilty party" David asked.

"If he's fool enough to come here and they get their hands on him he will be locked up for some time at least. And Romanian jails are not the best place in which to spend 15 years. Another beer Harry, David?"

"Not for me." Harry turned to David. "You stay and have another one. I'm going to go back and go through that quote again. Oh and I think that I'll miss dinner and have an early night. 'See you in the morning." Harry turned and left.

David dismissed the feeling of disappointment that he wouldn't have Harry's company for the rest of the evening and turned to George

"Thanks, I will take you up on that."

Siggie the German appeared and a few more beers later David was feeling a little light headed and thought that he would return to the hotel.

Bidding goodnight to the two of them, he walked the few steps to the end of the road and along Boulevard Magheru to the Theodore. Approaching the reception for his key, a sudden thought struck him.

"Is there a nice Romanian restaurant close by?" It was a spur of the moment thought. Why shouldn't he get a flavour of Bucharest instead of closeting himself in the Victorian decor of the Theodore for yet another night?"

"Yes sir, Restaurant Casa Dobra. It is just round the corner of the next street down towards Piati Universitatlii."

"Is it typically Romanian?"

"Yes sir. You will get a good meal there." The way he said a 'good meal' confirmed David's judgement that the meals in the Theodore restaurant were not good.

Deciding to give it a try, he left his key at the reception desk and set out for the restaurant which, following the directions, he soon found.

The view he got on entering was not quite what he had expected. It was more of a bar than a restaurant. There were some small uncovered tables, each having either two or four chairs tucked under them. The bar, if that was what it was, was almost empty except for two old men sitting at a table in the corner playing cards. One, wearing a sailor's cap looked up. The other, balancing a dark cigarette in the corner of his mouth, kept his attention on the cards.

The barman stopped polishing the glasses for a moment and looked enquiringly at David.

"Do you speak English? "

The barman shook his head.

Let's try a little German, David thought. "Kann Man hier essen?"

It worked. The barman pointed to some stairs in the corner leading down to a basement; David hadn't noticed them.

Still under gaze of the 'cap' and now ' the cigarette', David made his way across the room and went down the stairs. The basement had been fashioned to look like a cave with the walls cemented and painted into rugged cave-like contours.

Not bad, were his first thoughts. Then he noticed that the tablecloths had a droopy look. Starch hadn't yet reached Romania.

A waiter came forward and beckoned him to a table; when he was seated he handed him a menu card. David's heart sank. It was in Romanian. "English ?" He tried again. The waiter shook his head.

"Deutsch?"

This got more response. The waiter scurried back to a little table in the corner and re-appear with another menu, this time

65

in German. Hopefully there will be something he could recognise. Whoopee! Schnitzel Romanischer Zigeuner Art. Now that was something he could understand. A pork steak grilled and piled up with a spicy topping. He'd tried it in Austria, although here it might have a Romanian flavour.

He pointed to the entry. "OK?" The waiter nodded. Now he could try ordering some wine.

"Weiss Wein bitte?" Again a nod. He was feeling very pleased with himself. Suddenly he noticed a rather tall young man, about his own age, getting up from the table on the other side of the restaurant and making his was way towards him.

"Hello. You are English?" Can I help you?"

Slightly intoxicated with his success in ordering the whole meal in German, he replied with typical British politeness.

"That's very kind of you, but I managed to order using my little smattering of German." He liked the sound of that and hoped it didn't sound too smug.

"Yes I heard you. You have ordered the same as I." David noted the formal reply but was impressed with the flow. "May I join you? I would like very much to hear English."

This was really what David had hoped for. Some personal contact with the Romanians.

"Please do. It will be nice to have company."

The newcomer said something to the waiter who nodded; then he sat down in the chair opposite David.

"My name is Gheorghe, Gheorghe Petrescu." He was surprised to hear such an English name, George. In was only later that he learnt that it was spelled differently.

"David, David Edwards."

"You are here on business?" A red light flashed for the moment. Should he really be talking to this man?

Without waiting for an answer, Gheorghe continued, "I am a footballer – full back. I play for the University." He smiled. David breathed a sigh of relief. Perhaps he was seeing too many reds under the bed. But he had been warned.

"You have very many good football clubs in England. I like Bobbie Moore. He is a great centre back. Do you play?"

"No, but I follow West Ham. Have you heard of West Ham?"

"West Ham, but of course – Jeff Hurst and the world cup. I also like Manchester United."

"Everybody seems to like Man. United," said David a little bitterly.

The meals arrived and it was, as David expected, pork with lots of spicy mixture, topped with mushrooms.

"Do you say 'good appetite' in England?"

"Not very often, but we'll break the rules as we're in Romania. "Guten Appetit"

The wine arrived and, since there were already two glasses on the table, David offered one to his dining companion. It was received with obvious pleasure.

"I expect to go to Wembley in March, that is if I am picked for the party to go with the national team. We have a friendly match against England. It will be an experience for me but I will not have a chance to see anything as we fly in the day before and fly out the day after the match."

"That's a shame because I could have met up with you and shown you something of London." David prided himself on knowing London as his father had often taken him to see the sites of the capital when he was a young lad. For a fleeting moment David recollected how much his father had done for him.

They chatted on, Gheorghe was careful not to talk about politics. He explained that although he was a student at the University, this was really a backhanded method of paying him to play football, which was supposed only to be played at amateur level.

The meal was good and the wine not bad.

As he finished his Romanian spicy bread pudding, a sweet that his companion had recommended him to try, Gheorghe suddenly made a suggestion.

"Now we are finished, why do you not join me and my friends at the Corinthian Palace? There is some good music and dancing."

David had already seen this hotel. It wasn't far from the Theodore.

"OK as long as I won't be intruding."

He beckoned to the waiter and made the writing motion, the international sign for asking for the bill. This duly arrived and, converting to pounds sterling at 25 Lei to the pound, it worked out to about £3.50. Not bad.

"Can I pay for your meal?" At that sort of price David could afford to throw his money about!

"I do not pay," smiled Gheorghe, who went on to explain that as a member of the national team squad he was entitled to a few privileges such as free restaurant meals.

Having paid, they walked in the cool night air to the Corinthian Palace where, true enough, there was a band playing Romanian music to which couples were dancing. The dancing reminded him of the nights at the Saalbacherhof during his Austrian holiday. There the couples sort of jigged about, rather than danced. Give him the quickstep any old time: a chassis here and a fishtail there. He was in his element on a dance floor, but this was foreign to him in more ways than one.

One of the young ladies invited him to dance, but he declined and sat just enjoying the music and the atmosphere. What impressed him most was all the unconcerned and friendly touching that went on between the boys and the girls and even between the boys and the boys. It showed a real affection between them.

He'd been served a beer and, although he couldn't join in the conversation, somehow he made some sort of communication with Gheorghe's friends. Everything was going serenely when he noticed Gheorghe standing on the edge of the dance floor talking to someone of about his own age or slightly older, in a manner very different from that which Gheorghe had shown so far. The conversation looked intense and slightly secretive.

They parted and Gheorghe came back to the table, smiling again.

"Do you like it here?"

"Yes," replied David. "It's nice of you to ask me to join you and meet your friends. They seem a nice lot of lads and lasses."

"Sorry, 'lads and lasses', I do not know these words." His face wrinkled quizzically.

"I'm sorry, it's not really good English. I mean young men and young women."

The smile was back. David noticed that Gheorghe had a small packet wrapped up in newspaper in his hand. He estimated it to be about six by eight by three inches. Turning round, Gheorghe appeared to catch the eye of someone at the far side of the room. He waved then turned back.

"Excuse me I see someone I must speak to," and with that he got up, placed the package on the table, and begun to make his way over to his colleague.

One by one everyone left the table and David realised that he was now the only one left sitting at the table with the package. He couldn't even see any of Gheorghe's young friends. He frantically looked at the people on the dance floor to see if he could locate a familiar face. Neither Gheorghe nor his friends were anywhere to be seen. The music seemed to tail off and there was a strange sort of hush around him.

Only then did a red light flash in David's mind. He felt a certain uneasiness about the package, whatever it contained. Should he just dismiss the incident, or was there more behind the sudden disappearance of everyone who was with him at the table just minutes ago?

Reds under the bed or not, David knew it was time to go, but how could he leave without being noticed? He felt certain that they had tried to lure him into some kind of compromising situation.

The music started up again and he could see some of the young people now sitting at other tables. Gheorghe himself had apparently disappeared. The parcel seemed to grow larger the more he looked at it.

His fear increased when he thought he saw the Romanian to whom Gheorghe had been talking, glancing over in his direction.

There was something disturbing about him; although he was in civilian clothes his stance was that of an official.

Chapter 6

"Hi." A voice suddenly broke into his thoughts. Turning, he saw Siggie.

"Siggie, tell me I am wrong but you see that package there…" David related how it came to be there.

Siggie listened carefully, his normally smiling face becoming increasingly serious. When David had finished his story, there was a short pause. Siggie pulled up a chair and sat down. "I think that you have understood the situation correctly but don't worry for the moment. They will not make any more moves whilst I am here. I suggest that we carry on talking then in few minutes you get up and look around and I will point to the toilets over there. Casually you will make you way first in the direction of the toilet then when you are half-way there, turn right and leave by the exit over there." David looked in the direction of the nod of his head and noticed that the toilets were past the hotel exit.

"I will stay here until you have gone, then slip back to the chick that I am trying to lay tonight" His American and his stated intentions gave David just a flicker of amusement.

Taking his time, David got up and looked around as if looking for a toilet. Siggie did his bit and David made his way slowly, first towards the toilets, and then to the exit. Once there he quickened his steps and made for the nearest sanctuary, which was the Embassy Club.

George Fox was still there. Apparently it was his duty night. David, looking a little sheepish, related what had happened.

"You did absolutely the right thing." David was relieved to hear this.

"But what's behind it all?"

"It may not have been planned from the start but I bet that you were identified by a party member and by the secret police. They saw the opportunity to compromise you by charging you with smuggling western cigarettes into the country. The penalty for your release would be a drop in the contract prices being negotiated. You would have been helpless to do anything but comply with their requirements. I have no doubt that this Gheorghe was a genuine person but that is what Communism does to you."

"Phew. That was a lucky escape then." Suddenly David noticed that he was sweating, even though the temperature in the Club was quite low. Sheila and the intimacy he'd enjoyed with her seemed to be a pleasant far-off memory. He declined the offer of a beer and made his way back to the hotel where he hurried to the sanctuary, if it was a sanctuary, of his suite. Sleep did not come easily, but eventually he managed to leave the world and drift into a troubled sleep.

He awoke early and, not having arranged to meet Harry until 8.30 for breakfast, lay awake in bed recalling the events of the previous evening. At least the tale would be worth a few beers when he related it to the boys back home. The interpretation that George at the Embassy Club had put on it seemed unbelievable, but then it also seemed incredible that for merely passing on commercial information to a potential supplier a minister could face a firing squad. Trading information must happen nearly all the time in British politics. In Britain if it were discovered that someone had received a kick back, then there may be a scandal, perhaps a court case and at worst a short stretch in prison – but the death penalty. It didn't seem real to David. Finally his train of thoughts came to a halt and he leisurely showered and shaved. At least there was room to move about in the suite, unlike the pokey room in the Aerial at Heathrow.

Having packed his briefcase with product information, he left for the breakfast room. While he waited for Harry to arrive, he was twice approached by the waiter who asked him if his choice was coffee or tea (hot water and a tea bag, as he had already experienced). Eventually, out of embarrassment, he ordered coffee and set about the stale bread, which he improved with butter and jam. Eight thirty came and went and, by nine o'clock having finished his breakfast, he felt that he ought to check if Harry was on his way. Leaving the breakfast room, he made his way to the reception.

"Can I telephone Room 312 from here?"

"Room 312? Mr Robson checked out earlier this morning to catch the 8.30 flight to Zurich."

Checked out! Checked out! David couldn't believe what he heard.

"Are you sure it was Mr Robson who checked out?"

"Yes sir. Oh, and by the way, there is a telex for you Mr Edwards. It arrived a few minutes ago."

Still completely confused, he took the coarse piece of paper to the reception area where he could sit down and read it. He looked quickly at the sender's name: Mr P.J. Osbourne, K.M. Industrial Ltd.

```
Dear David

Harry has had to return home suddenly to deal with
a domestic situation. He tells me that you have
already accompanied him in the negotiations at
Romconstructimpex and Romchemimpex, so please can
you continue with the meetings arranged for today?
For your information the FFs are 486 and 940,
respectively.

There is also a need for you to go to the
Romchemimpex Technical Bureau in Brasov tomorrow -
Friday - to receive a schedule for the delivery of
Krone Chemicals procurement order for K4 Ageing
Agents. They use it in their rubber products.

They will tell you what they want but you must not
commit Krone to start before January. The Bucharest
office knows that you are going, so they may
mention it. When the negotiations are completed
get a map from them to help you find the office. It
is in Calea Unirii. Ask for Mr Deutmann. My advice
is to get to Brasov and find a taxi rank and take a
taxi. Your appointment is not until 12.00, so you
have time to get there if you leave shortly after
8.00.
```

```
The last visit in Romania is on Monday at Resita
for a meeting at the Locomotive works with their
design people. We have a chance to get specified on
a new range of locomotives with Priory Paints'
heat-resisting quality base paint. PP reference
4217HR. You'll find all the specs in the Manual.

They need details to write into the procurement
spec. Mr Dinicu Mihail is your contact. Your
appointment on Monday is at 14.00. You are booked
in at the Hotel Comercial in the Main Square on
Monday night for your return on Tuesday. We are
arranging for your tickets to be sent to you for
your flight to Budapest on Wednesday. Harry will
meet you at Budapest airport.

I am sorry that we are asking you to cover these
visits but to go back again to Romania would be
costly. I know you can cope and I have the utmost
confidence in you.

Best regards

Peter Osbourne

DIRECTOR

P.S. Harry has left the keys to the 1800 at the
reception for you to pick up.
```

'Utmost confidence indeed,' thought David. 'I wish that I had the utmost bloody confidence.'

He went back to the beginning of the telex.

'– FFs are 485 and 940, respectively –'It threw him at first, then he remembered Harry's explanation "I should have mentioned that the final final prices, that is the so called final reduction, has already been agreed with Priory Paints."

So that explains the 'FF' but what about the numbers?

He went back up to his room and pulled out the copies of the two quotations that they had discussed. The quote for Romchemimpex was for £2.31 per kilo and Harry had reduced this to £2.19p per kilo. He was going to make a 'final final' offer, but how does that tie up to 486?

For a moment he felt quite alone. His uneventful life at Arkus now seemed very attractive, but there was nothing he could do about that now. He racked his brains, attempting to recall anything else that Harry had told him.

'When we get prices back, he (Peter Osbourne) will come back with the authority for us to make a slightly lower offer of a further 5%. Romchemimpex will most likely know of this before we will, because they will get the copy of the telex sent to Harry.' David also recalled that Harry had said, 'I will pretend to be totally dejected and concede a further 3%.'

David did his sums. £2.31 less 5% less 5% and then less a further 3%. That equalled £2.02.

Back to school. If $x = y$, and x equalled 2.02 and $y = 486$, then x must have a factor f, but what factor?

Say $f = 486/2.02 = 240$.

Of course! David suddenly realised that Peter Osbourne had given him the final offer in old pennies. There were 240 old pennies to the pound before decimalisation. It didn't take him long to work out the 'final final' for Romchemimpex. He felt elated, almost slightly intoxicated. He'd cracked a code.

His 'high' was interrupted by the ring of the telephone. It made him jump. Who could be calling him?

"Hello?"

"Hello, David?" It was a familiar English voice. George Fox, British Embassy. "David I believe that you have a meeting with two enterprises today. What time is the first appointment?"

"The first one is at 10.30." David answered.

"Can you pop in to see me before you go. Preferable straight away if you can," and then, as if to ward of any questions, "I will explain things when you get here – just a few points that I'd like to clear up about your visits." Before he could reply there was the click of the receiver being replaced.

David checked that he hadn't left anything round his room, made sure that he had everything he needed for the two meetings and left for the short walk to the embassy.

Again he passed the khaki-uniformed soldier. "Gosh! how scruffy they all appeared, with their ill-fitting uniforms," he thought and approached the main building. The embassy was typically Eastern European, with high narrow windows and French doors. There was no blanket here. Inside was a neat reception desk, manned by an attractive young lady who seemed to be expecting him.

"Mr Edwards?" His heart sank. The voice had a Romanian accent. There would be no chance of getting to know her better, something he would have liked. If he had been at home he would have made at least two of his girl friends happy in this period, besides doing himself a bit of good.

" Mr Fox is expecting you. Would you come this way."

He followed her up the winding balustrade stairs to tall double doors, similar to those at the other buildings he had visited in Bucharest. They opened into a high ornate-ceiling room.

Seated at a large office table at one end was George, who got up as soon as David entered.

"Hello David. Good of you to come." David reflected again that that wasn't a Dagenham accent, more like Harrow or Eaton. But the smile was genuine.

"Sit down. Tea or coffee? It is real tea – out of a tea pot." The warm reception made him feel more at ease.

"Tea please" He seated himself in one of the comfortable studded leather chairs, thankful that he didn't have to sit in one of those armchairs where you couldn't really sit up straight and had to perch on the edge.

"I understand that Harry has gone back." George having ordered some tea for them both, looked serious.

"Yes. Apparently he had to deal with a domestic problem. He must have been upset because he didn't contact me before he left for the early morning SwissAir flight." There was a pregnant pause. Again George's expression was serious.

"David, this is confidential. You remember that I mentioned that Golescu, the Minister for Construction, had been executed?" David nodded. "Well, in our diplomatic bag yesterday we received details of the background to the affair." George seemed to gather his breath before proceeding.

"It appears that it came to light that he had been receiving Western currency for passing on information about forthcoming projects to a Western supplier. At the moment we don't know any more than that. What we do know is that instructions have been issued to all Romanian commercial units to try to find out who was the recipient of the information, the western supplier."

"But what will happen if they find out who was receiving the information?"

"He will be tried for spying or for corruption of an official and jailed, for at least some time."

"How does that affect me?" David was becoming worried.

"All the commercial units will be trying to please their Lords and Masters and doing their utmost to find the offender."

"But I have no connection with this Ministry?"

"No. But the fact that Harry has, it would seem, 'disappeared suddenly ', this might mean that they put some pressure on you. I must admit that I don't like the look of it either. If Harry was mixed up in it, then he's a fool, but it is not our place to jump to conclusions."

David suddenly remembered the visit to the August 23 works that he and Harry had made – 'You heard of the expected new project for the Boiler Plant then' and Harry's reply, 'Yes. I was lucky enough to ask the right questions at the right time.' David wondered if this implicated Harry.

"What should I do?"

"Nothing, but be very careful. If any questions are asked you know nothing of the matter; give the impression that you don't want to know anything either. Watch out for any approaches from people other than the business contacts."

It's like being in a monastery, thought David. George now relaxed a little. "Nothing to worry about then." The tea arrived. It was real English tea, poured from a china teapot by George and accompanied by some McVitae digestive biscuits." We have them flown over in the diplomatic bag." George had pre-empted my question.

"Are you going to come to the film show tonight? We have a James Bond – something about Russia, but it will be a break from the boredom of Bucharest. Incidentally, Carol asked me if I knew why you dashed off yesterday evening. I didn't go into details, but I think that she was disappointed."

Carol? Oh yes. David remembered. She was standing by George when Harry first introduced them. His recollection of her was favourable. Things were looking up. At least it took away some of the apprehensions that he had been feeling a few minutes before.

"Well, you had better be off for your first meeting. It's with Romconstructimpex – Mr Alexandru isn't it?" David nodded. I'll get Catrina to organise you a taxi. We will see you tonight then?"

As they shook hands, David confirmed that he would be pleased to come. One of the tall doors opened and the Romanian receptionist announced that a taxi was waiting.

Chapter 7

David was again struck by the blanket approach to keeping heat in. He pushed the blanket aside and found himself in the now-familiar smoky atmosphere. He surmised that the air never changed from one month to another. David went up to the desk and explained that he had a meeting with Mr Alexandru. After a few minutes Mrs Fiore appeared. He knew that he could not bring himself to go through Harry's hand kissing act. Instead he proffered a hand, which Mrs Fiore gripped very limply, with only a trace of a smile on her face.

"Mr Robson is not with you?"

"No, he had to go back to England to deal with a domestic matter. It was very urgent so he didn't have a chance to ring and tell you that I would be continuing our negotiations."

There was no response. Mrs Fiore turned and started to walk away. He assumed that he was supposed to follow her. She led him to the same sparsely furnished room. Mr Alexandru was already sitting on the other side of the large table but this time there was another man beside him.

"Good morning Mr Edwards." Mr Alexandru got up and offered a hand, which was not very much firmer than Mrs Fiore's.

"May I introduce Mr Ionescu. Mr Ionescu is our General Manager." The man next to Mr Alexandru nodded gravely.

"Good morning." David responded, not quite knowing why he should be getting the VIP treatment. Alexandru motioned him to sit down.

"I am sorry that Mr Robson cannot be here, but he had to return to England to deal with an urgent domestic matter."

"What sort of domestic matter?" The enquiry was blunt. Mr Ionescu questioned David in perfect English

"I'm afraid I don't know. It was so urgent that he had to leave early to catch the plane and he only left me the details for our meeting."

"You have been to other meetings in Bucharest?" Again it was Ionescu questioning him.

"Yes to Romchemimpex."

"And other places?"

David could feel himself becoming a little hot around the collar.

"Only to the August 23 Works."

"Why did you go there?"

"I'm afraid I don't know the reason. Mr Robson met someone. I think that it was just a courtesy call." He wondered if they used that expression in Romania.

"You seemed to be very successful in securing contracts for your principals?" Mr Ionescu leaned forward as he asked the question. David didn't know how to respond, so he waited for the next question. He noticed that Mrs Fiore seemed to be uncomfortable in Mr Ionescu's presence.

"How have you been so successful?"

"I suppose it's because we have good products and competitive prices."

"You also appear to be the first company to get in your quotations after the tenders are issued."

David could feel that there was some hidden agenda here, but exactly what they were trying to get him to say eluded him. However, he knew that he needed to say something.

"Well, our company is always keen to secure your business and I know that they always give your enquiries priority."

This appeared to satisfy him and, to David's relief, Mr Alexandru turned to the subject of the prices.

"At our last meeting you were told that we could not accept £2.31 and that you could only cut this by 5%. That is not good enough. Have you been in contact with your Mr Osbourne?" If Harry was right, and he had no reason to doubt him, they knew bloody well that he'd been in touch with Peter Osbourne.

"Yes, he has discussed the matter with Priory Paints and, with some difficulty, they have agreed that we can offer a further

5%. I think you'll agree that this makes our offer very attractive, considering your inflation."

"You keep on talking of this inflation." This was Mr Ionescu talking. "Last time you spoke of the hotel prices in Romania and the taxi fare."

How did he know that we spoke about inflation when he wasn't at the last meeting? Either he was well briefed or there was a 'bug' in the room. David paused. Was he getting paranoid? Putting this to the back of his mind, he returned to the negotiation.

"Mr Ionescu," (always use the person's name when you want to make an important statement Alfred Tack had said), "the initial offer was a good one, and we have already reduced the price twice for you. I can't go any lower."

"How much does it cost you to visit us? "Mr Alexandru was now back 'in the frame'.

"I'm afraid I don't know." David's company, K.M., bought the air tickets.

"Then I will tell you. Your ticket cost 280 English pounds and you are here for two weeks?" David nodded.

"You will spend another 100 English pounds in Bucharest; that is the cost of hotel, your cost of food and ..." David thought that he saw a faint smile appear when he added "and the cost of the taxis." Where was all this leading?

"Mr Edwards,"(had Mr Alexandru learned Alfred Tack's tactics as well?) "we cannot get permission to pay this price this week." he looked at Mr Ionescu who nodded. "So you will have to leave without the signed contract and return at a later date to conclude the negotiation if we cannot agree a price today. How will Priory Paints feel about paying the extra cost incurred if you have to return?" Now it was clear. Make a further reduction or go away empty handed.

"You are placing me in a very difficult position, Mr Alexandru. I have no authority to make further reductions. If I do take it upon myself to reduce the price any further, Mr Osbourne may be unhappy with the deal, in spite of the fact that you seem to be making very good sense." A little flattery may help.

"But Mr Edwards," there was a sound of triumph in his voice now. "You will be saving the company money if you concede just a further 5%."

"That is out of the question," replied David, thinking that he should show some resistance. To emphasis the point he started to gather up his papers. It did the trick. Now to reach the final final.

"Could we get a 3% reduction approved this afternoon?" David was surprised that the question was put by Mr Ionescu to Mr Alexandru. After a slight pause, Mr Alexandru nodded.

"So, Mr Edwards, you have the opportunity to take home a valuable contract with just a further adjustment of 3%."He looked down at the paper and pencilled in some figures.

"I calculate that makes the price £2.02. Shall we get the contract prepared?"

That was it! The 'asking for the order' close. They really were clued up on selling techniques or, in this case, buying techniques.

'Put on a totally dejected act.' David remembered Harry's words.

"Mr Alexandru, if there is no other way, I will accept the order at £2.02, but this may mean that this will be the last time that I will be here. Can I wait while you get the contract finalised?"

"Certainly." It was all smiles now, as if there had been no problems. "I will arrange some coffee whilst we are waiting." Mrs Fiore had left the room with the instructions for the preparation of the contract.

"By the way, do you know that our National team is playing Wales next month?"

Wales? David thought quickly. "Yes but they will have to stop JPR from running away with it."

The smiles broadened.

"Now. How are you enjoying your visit to Bucharest? Have you seen much of our city?"

"No. In fact, except for visiting a restaurant I have not been anywhere other than to the Embassy Club."

"But you should try to see something of our city before your go home." David could hardly believe that this was the same person talking as just a few minutes ago. Now they were both full of smiles.

"You are here on Saturday?" David nodded.

"You should visit Parcul Herăstrău, It is a large park, but in the park we have assembled all the old houses from all over Romania. You will find it very interesting."

"How do I get there – take a taxi?"

No, no, they are too expensive." That was a laugh coming from Mr Alexandru. "You can go by bus. I will write the address down for you and if you show it to the Tarom man in your hotel, he will tell you which bus to take and where to pick it up. Then if you show it to the conductor on the bus, she will tell you when to get off."

The Turkish coffee had now arrived. David was surprised that he was beginning to get to like it, as long as he remembered to stop drinking before he reached the thick sludge in the bottom of the small cup. Mrs Fiore had also returned with the contract, which gave the price as £2.02. David hoped that all the other conditions were the same but, remembering that Harry had said that you could trust them to be honest once the price was agreed, he signed and dated the copy and gave it to them. Further smiles, warm handshakes all round and then he was off.

Once out in boulevard Dinicu Golescu, he could hardly believe that he had done it. He had carried out negotiations with an obviously experienced group of negotiators and come out with exactly what he (and Priory Paints) wanted. Where had he been up until now? He was a professional! The feeling of satisfaction was very exhilarating. David almost felt like shouting but, dragging himself back down to earth, he remembered that he now had to do it all over again with Romchemimpex. He could remember the way to their offices in Calea Grivitei; it took about 10 minutes on foot.

When David saw the building for the second time, he thought that it looked even more Victorian than before. The ornateness of the doorway and the panelled interior reminded him of some of the museum buildings in London that his father had taken him to visit as a child. Again the receptionist kept him waiting, looking at him as if he were, as his mother would have put it, 'something that the cat had brought in'.

"Comrade Ilescu, please. David Edwards, K.M. Industrial."

Still without a smile, she announced his arrival. However, all that changed when the delightful Matti appeared in the office doorway. The smile slipped a little when she saw that David was alone; Harry was not with him. Before she could ask, David explained that Harry had had to return home to deal with a domestic situation. Either hiding her disappointment, or satisfied that nothing untoward had happened to him, she proceeded to escort David to the same room as before.

Mr Ilescu was there together with Mr Coman plus another rather tallish, even distinguished one might say, grey-haired gentleman. It was he who made the first move.

"Come in Mr Edwards." The English was good but there was a slight accent. David could not place it. He shook hands with Mr Ilescu, who looked a little apprehensive, perhaps because of the presence of another person. Matti, feeling that she should establish her position as an interpreter, made the introductions.

"This is Mr Dieter, our General Manager."

Not again, thought David.

Dieter interrupted his thoughts.

"We can talk in English Mr Edwards. In fact, we can talk in plain English. Mr Ilescu has told me the prices that you have offered. I understand that you went back to your Mr Osbourne to make him see reason.

"Yes Mr Dieter, and reluctantly he has agreed that I can offer a further 5% reduction on the prices that Mr Robson offered. That really does bring the price down to a very attractive figure."

"But not attractive enough." Matti and Mr Ilescu were looking a little uncomfortable.

"How much do you think your visit to us has cost?"

They've all got the same script, thought David, but he decided that there was nothing for it but to play out the charade. With almost a repeat performance of the previous negotiation, the drama was performed. David secretly felt very excited when he put on his dejected 'perhaps this is the last time that I will be here' look. The formalities over, Mr Ilescu organised the coffee. It was David's turn to make conversation.

"Tell me Mr Dieter. Where did you learn such good English?"

"Before the war, in my school in Leipzig."

"You are not Romanian then?"

"No, I came here five years ago to take up this position, but whether I stay here is the question. How do you say it in Shakespeare's language? 'To be or not to be here, that is the question'." He smiled proudly.

David tried to look admiring, but he couldn't help noticing that Matti was no longer smiling. The coffee duly drunk and the contract signed, he bade his leave. Matti, with almost a wistful look, saw him back to the reception and said goodbye.

As he stepped out into the boulevard again, he felt slightly weary, so he decided that he would go back to the hotel, have a beer, then take a cat nap until it was time to go down for the evening meal. 'Don't ever choose the hamburgers,' he remembered Harry telling him.

The beer wasn't bad but he was distracted by the loud voice of a German who was on the phone. David couldn't help but listen, but he did not grasp all the meaning. However, he could guess from some of the words – 'Skonto' and 'unrealistisch' and the hysterical tone of the man that he was obviously being pushed by the Romanians for a further discount in some contract.

David was feeling rather pleased with himself, and the overheard conversation kept him amused while he drunk his beer. When he had finished, he wandered up to his suite, slipped off his clothes, and got under the sheets for a nap. When he awoke he was surprised to find he'd been asleep for more than an hour and a half and it was nearly 6 p.m.

A good shower helped to bring him fully awake. Then he made his way quickly down to the restaurant, noting again the 1920's decor styles in the corridors and public rooms as he passed through them. Again, he chose the pork, which was served with a sauce and chips. He also ordered a carafe of wine, which from his previous experience at the outside restaurant, was the best thing he had found since his arrival in Bucharest.

After some wait, the meal arrived; as usual the meat was almost cold and the chips were greasy. But he was hungry, so he tucked in. After the meal, he returned to his room. His intention was to go to the Embassy Club but, remembering that he had to find his way to Brasov the following day, he decided to settle down first with his Neville Shute, for some gentle relaxation. The stress of the day took its toll and he soon found that his eyelids were getting heavy, so he decided not to make the visit to the Embassy Club, but to have an early night.

Chapter 8

David slept well. Perhaps the satisfaction of having successfully concluded the negotiations helped. Looking at his watch, he noticed that it was already a quarter to seven – 'leave at 8.00'. He remembered the instruction in the telex from Peter Osbourne. He'd have to get a move on if he was to leave on time. He showered and shaved as quickly as he could. Packing up his briefcase so that he wouldn't have to return to the room after breakfast, he hurriedly descended the balustrade staircase and went into the restaurant.

Seating himself as close to the waiters' table as he could, he tried to catch the attention of one of them. Irritatingly, he was ignored for about ten minutes. Even after ordering, it still took a further five minutes for his orange juice and instant coffee (no milk) to arrive. There was a further wait before the semi-stale bread, unsalted butter and thick jam was put on the table. Eating quickly, David managed to finish and be out of the restaurant by just after 8 o'clock. The reception again was empty. When the receptionist finally appeared, David asked him for the key to the 1800, which he had been told had been left there by Harry. The receptionist stared at him blankly.

"You say it was left here?"

'Oh no!' thought David, 'not another fiasco'. However things were not so bad this time; four more people were brought in to search for the key and it magically appeared.

"Enjoy your trip to Brasov," commented the receptionist as the keys were passed over.

Hold on, thought David. How did he know where I was going? Then he remembered the long telex from Peter Osbourne. Even the receptionists had read it. Ah well, who cares if they know; it was not a trade secret. Nevertheless it irritated him. Making his way down to the underground garage, David started to relax. In fact he was beginning to get rather excited at the thought that he would see a little of Romania, other than Bucharest. The Morris 1800 was standing alone in the large car park. He had only driven one once before, and David couldn't help but think how much larger it was than his Marina. The thought of his old Marina made his mind drift back to Sheila and their antics in the back of the car. Maybe things could have developed further if he'd had the spacious 1800. His abstinence was beginning to tell.

David turned the key and the engine purred into action. Gingerly, wary of driving the large 1800, he made his way out on to Boulevard Magheru and turned north to the airport, constantly reminding himself to keep to the right-hand side of the road. He had looked at the map the night before and knew that at some point he would have to turn off to pick up Route 7 and then Route 71. The 1800 ran well. He enjoyed the large seats; the driving position was different from that of the Marina, but it was very comfortable and gave good all-round vision.

In the short time he had been in Bucharest, he'd noticed that there were very few vehicles on the road – in the city there were mostly taxis but as he left the outskirts these became fewer in number and the passing traffic was mostly commercial vehicles.

Within half an hour the main road narrowed and he was out in the countryside with large fields each side. With so little traffic on the road, he was free to take in the scenery and was struck by the size of the fields that seemed to stretch for miles; cultivated fields were slowly replaced by fields full of large sunflowers.

Now, the passing traffic was peppered with tractors pulling farm carts. At certain points the air was filled with a distinctly agricultural smell; the origin of this was obviously the manure that he could see being spread on the newly ploughed fields. Although it was quite chilly outside, a little wintry sunshine peaked through emphasising the big yellow petals of the sunflowers. They were much larger than sunflowers that he had seen before and they presented a colourful sight. The country scene changed as he approached a built-up area with a few buildings; it looked more like a village than a town. David could see a queue of tractors ahead and, on approaching, he could see that they were being held up by a barrier guarding a train crossing. He passed a sign, 'CRÂNGAŞI', and soon after he drove across the level crossing the number of buildings beside the road dwindled and he was once again out on the open road.

Perhaps his decision to take this job had not been a bad one. He was certainly seeing much more than he would if he were trundling backwards and forwards around the London North Circular. His mind wandered back over the different experiences that he had had since leaving the UK. Somehow at that moment, as he was driving a comfortable car along uncongested roads, the bad ones didn't seem quite so bad. The weak rays of sunshine shone through the windows and warmed the interior a little. He wondered what 'the boys' would be doing this weekend. It occurred to him how pathetic some of them were, on those Saturday nights, trying their luck to pick-up a girl at the Palais, but usually going home alone. For a moment he felt a slight pang of regret that he had not valued Sheila more. At the time he'd just been looking for sexual satisfaction.

The car ran very smoothly and, even though the road was quite narrow for a main road, he was making good time. At this rate he would reach Brasov very early. He would have time for a stop and a coffee at the next town or village.

The sign for TÂRGOVISTE appeared and shortly afterwards the road passed through the town with its collection of different buildings. Wending his way through the narrow road at what appeared to be the end of the town, he was once again out into the country. The need to concentrate on his driving had broken his reveries and he turned his attention to the road.

After a further 15 minutes or so he was presented with another sign, which read PIATUSCU. David looked at his watch. He had been making good time, so he thought that he would stop for a cup of coffee. Driving into the town, he came to a square where there were places to park. Luckily too, there was a hotel that appeared to have a bar on the ground floor. He stopped the car, got out, and walked the few yards across the road to the net covered glass door of what was either a bar or restaurant. He was relieved to see that this door wasn't backed by a blanket! However, the acrid smell of cigarette smoke still hit him as he entered the room.

Looking around he found an empty small table in the corner. As he seated himself he noticed that he had drawn the attention of a swarthy skinned group of men who were standing at the bar. The older one, who David guessed was about 60 years old, was seated on a stool, whilst the others stood and were holding small glasses of rose coloured drink. The waitress behind the bar looked up but made no attempt to come over to serve him. After taking some time to meticulously polish a glass, she finally came over to serve him.

She said something in Romania; it meant nothing to David but he guessed that she was asking him what he wanted.

"Café?" David made the sign of holding a saucer and drinking from an imaginary cup.

This prompted another flow of Romanian. David guessed that she was asking whether he wanted something further. He nodded that he did. Yet a further question. Well ! In for a penny in for a pound, and David nodded again. This seemed to satisfy the waitress; she turned away and busied herself with the coffee machine, returning with the traditional Turkish black coffee.

Hardly had he started to sip his coffee when she returned with a plate on which was a thick chunk of unbuttered bread, some blue and very white cheese and a tomato. The cheese smelled strong but he decided to give it a try. It tasted very salty but by accompanying it with bites of the tomato, which was very juicy, he found it quite palatable. He recognised it as goat's cheese; he had had it once before, on that fateful skiing holiday in Austria.

Sipping his coffee, he noticed that the small group at the bar were still watching him, but none of them made any attempt to approach him. Suddenly the outside door of bar opened and two blue uniformed men in shallow peaked caps quickly entered and made their way towards him. Both carried revolvers.

"Papier?" demanded the older one. For the moment David was nonplussed. However, these were obviously people in some sort of authority, so he stood up and said "Excuse me?"

"Papier?" Repeated the older uniformed man again, whilst the other menacingly toyed with the handle of his revolver. David begun to comprehend – papier – papers – passport. Slowly sliding his hand into his inside pocket, he pulled out his passport and handed it to the uniformed man who opened it and started to thumb through the pages. His companion remained standing in the same position. David noticed that now he was all alone in the bar. The group that had been at the bar, including the older man who had been sitting on the stool, had all disappeared.

Closing the passport. The older official beckoned David to accompany him out of the bar. David complied, he did not know what this was all about, but he was aware of the officer with his hand still firmly on his revolver. Once outside the bar, the officer held David's arm firmly and led him across the road to a building with three or four concrete steps leading to a large door. Unsurprisingly, behind the door the doorway was covered with the inevitable thick blanket.

Pushed through the blanket, David was led across the foyer to another room. Immediately in front of him was a desk with a chair occupied by another blue uniformed man but this time he had no hat. Was this Mr Big?

Without a word, David was pushed towards a chair opposite Mr Big, and the older official handed him David's passport. He glanced through the pages without comment and, after some time, he looked up.

"You are English?"

David thought that it was rather a stupid question as his passport had Great Britain printed all over it.

"Yes."

"And why are you here?" Well, one thing was certain, he hadn't read David's telexes.

"Business. Visiting enterprises in Bucharest for contract negotiations."

"Then why are you in PIATUSCU?"
"I am going to Brasov."
"Why are you going to Brasov?"
"I am visiting Romchemimpex Technical Bureau in Brasov."
"Who are you seeing at Romchemimpex?"

David could feel himself beginning to panic. The telex was with his papers in the car.

"Er. The chap who deals with specifications." He was stalling.

"His name?" Damn it, David, think." He struggled to remember the man's name.

"Mr Deutmann," he blurted out.

Mr Big then snapped out some order to the young man who hurriedly left the room. There was silence whilst they all waited and Mr Big looked down and shuffled some papers. After some few minutes the young man re-appeared and reported to Mr Big.

"Mr Deutmann is expecting you at 12.00 noon. I suggest that you do not stop again on your journey."

And with that he went back to shuffling his papers. David was helped to his feet and lead back to the front entrance. He pushed his way out through the blanket and hurriedly crossed the road to his car.

Once back inside the car he started to breath more easily. He realised that he hadn't paid for his coffee. That could present more problems. Getting out of the 1800 once more, he entered the bar and approached the waitress who was polishing yet another glass. Rubbing his fingers together and miming the writing out of a bill, he indicated that he would like the bill. She scribbled something on her pad but, not bothering to read it, David put down a 10 Lei note and picked up the coins that she proffered in exchange.

Back at his car, he started the engine and drove off, with relief, at some speed. Once out on the open road he put his foot down and sped past more large fields, some with sunflowers and some being worked by Romanian women. He didn't stop until he reached the centre of Brasov.

Parking the car, he picked up his bag, locked the doors and made for the nearest taxi rank. He soon found it. There were three Dacia taxis waiting. He approached the first one in the line.

"Romchemimpex, Calea Unirii?"

The taxi driver nodded and David got in. Brasov, he noticed was not like Bucharest. The buildings were smaller and the streets appeared to be smaller than those in Bucharest. However, like Bucharest, there was little or no traffic – just a few taxis and the occasional bus. After about 10 minutes, during which time David had been able to re-read the telex from Peter Osbourne, the taxi pulled into a side street and stopped in front of a large building with iron gates. He wondered whether Mr Deutmann would be like the other contacts that he had met in Bucharest.

The taxi driver drew out a pad and wrote something. David used the same method as previously in dealing with written bills – a 10 Lei note worked the trick and he received some coins in return. Going through the iron gates, he noticed a large door with three steps. Two men, obviously not Romanians, were coming out. As they passed David, he recognised the language – German. David had noticed that there seemed to be quite a number of German salesmen looking for business in Romania.

Assuming that this was the main entrance for visitors, he went up the steps and pushed open the door. To his relief there was no blanket, only a very large reception hall with a window opening on to an office. Not surprisingly – he was getting used to the habit by now, the girl inside made no effort to acknowledge him when he knocked on the glass of the window. Eventually however she looked up and, without a glimmer of a smile, said "Da?"

"I have an appointment with Mr Deutmann," David handed her his card.

Silently she returned to her desk and muttered something into the telephone, and went back to her work. 'Thanks a bunch,' thought David, but realising that any reproach would be a waste of time, he moved away from the window and proceeded to examine the reception area a little further: a mosaic floor, cream walls green at the bottom, and a picture of a white coated worker in what appeared to be a laboratory. A door opened at the other side of the reception hall and a dark-haired woman, about 30 years old, approached him.

"Mr Edwards," a glimmer of a smile, "Mr Deutmann will see you now."

She turned and, without waiting to see if he was following her, went back out. David just caught the door as it was closing. He followed her down a passage until she stopped at a door on the right, which she opened and stood aside, beckoning him to enter. The room was not large and was furnished only with a desk and a small conference table. Getting up from the desk and moving forward to greet him as he entered was a small, rounded, bald headed man, who displayed a genuine broad smile.

"Mr Edwards. Please come in," he beckoned to a seat at the conference table. "It is very nice of you to come."

Quite taken aback, David slid into the seat, whereupon Deutmann took his place opposite.

"Coffee?"

"Thank you, yes." Deutmann nodded to the woman, who was still standing in the doorway. This was obviously a signal for her to go and organise the refreshments.

"I understand that you had a little trouble on route."

David remembered that the police had telephoned Romchemimpex.. Without waiting for a reply, Deutmann went on. "It was unfortunate that you chose to stop at Piatuscu. It is a little sensitive at the moment."

"Sensitive?"

"Yes, On account of the orphanage in the next village. A man was found trying to break into it and was shot trying to escape the police. But of course when you explained our meeting everything was all right."

That wasn't quite how David would have put it.

"Now, to business," another broad smile and then Deutmann proceeded to ask for the specifications to a number of Krone products. These were all listed in the larger spiral bound catalogue that David had taken over from Harry.

Thumbing through the pages, he came across a piece of paper in between one of the pages. What caught his attention was that it was the cheap paper that he had seen his Romanian contacts using at meetings for taking notes. He also noticed some handwriting on it that did not look to be in the western style of writing. He slipped the piece of paper into the back of the catalogue and carried on providing the information that Mr Deutmann had asked for. After about an hour, during which time the coffee had arrived and been consumed, they had finished discussing the Krone products in which Deutmann was interested.

"We shall specify these for the new project now that you have been kind enough to confirm the specifications. By the way how is Mr Robson?"

David explained why Mr Robson wasn't there and this seemed to satisfy Deutmann. With another broad smile he added that 'Mr Robson' was obviously very dedicated as he was always the first to contact them when there was a new project. Coincidentally, the dark haired woman returned at that moment and, with a warm handshake, he was despatched to the main entrance with the suggestion that he should return to Bucharest without stopping en route. A taxi had been called and Deutmann had arranged for the driver to be told the place to which David should be taken.

Back at the car, David paid the taxi, and got in, relieved to be on 'home territory', so to speak.

The journey home appeared to be longer, but perhaps that was just because of the tension that he had felt during the outward journey. Arriving on the outskirts of Bucharest, he went passed the turning to Otopeni Airport and continued straight on to the familiar surroundings of the Theodore.

Garaging the 1800, he made his way to his suite and felt grateful to be able to relax in his relatively luxurious room. After showering he went down to the restaurant, studied the same menu that he was given every evening, and chose the same meal – pork chops.

Chapter 9

The meal over, he signed the bill, with his room number, but then went back up to the suite. He wanted to collect his top coat to keep out the chill night air, but then he remembered the piece of paper that he'd found slipped into the Krone catalogue. He took the catalogue out of his briefcase and extracted the piece of paper.

There was no doubt in his mind that the originator of the writing on the piece of paper was not western. When he managed to decipher the information, he realised, with horror, that it contained details of the requirements for putting forward a successful proposal for a Krone product quotation.

So Harry was involved. David did not know whether he was the only one, but it explained his 'sudden disappearance'. He now had to decide whether he should share this information with George Fox. There had been a suggestion that there was a mole in the embassy, so David decided to say nothing.

As far as he was concerned, Harry had gone home to sort out a domestic problem. There was no reason to think that the piece of paper was incriminating, but it might be wise to dispose of it. David took it to the bathroom and proceeded to shred it into a dozen or so pieces and make sure that all the bits were safely flushed away. He could now put the matter out of his mind and concentrate on keeping himself out of trouble.

The five-minute stroll to the Embassy Club helped him to relax. He was looking forward to the James Bond film and meeting up with Carol again. He started to day-dream about Carol, basing his fantasies on past adventures with Sheila. He was obviously missing those close encounters. 'Don't rush in too fast,' David told himself, 'just lay the ground work for the next visit perhaps.' Although his thoughts were wandering, he was still conscious of footsteps coming up behind him. The footsteps quickened and someone appeared at his shoulder. Turning, David saw a middle-aged man dressed in an open-neck shirt under an ill-fitting coarse jacket. The man smiled.

"American?" the voice was accented.

"No. English." David decided to keep on walking.

"You have American or English money. I give you good rate for money."

David recalled the conversation on the plane when his travelling companion had warned him about the black market changing of currency – 'the person could be a police informer'.

"I'm sorry, I only have Romanian money." That did the trick. His walking companion stopped in his tracks leaving David, who kept on walking.

'Phew,' he thought. 'Another incident avoided.' He turned into the side street to the Embassy and found his path blocked by two khaki-uniformed men. "You have Romanian money?" The one on the left was speaking.

"Excuse me?"

"You have Romanian money?" The questioned was repeated.

"Yes but what's this all about?"

"You will show us all your Romanian money."

"Look here….," David began.

"Now." The second uniformed man had brought his carbine up and was pointing it at him.

David had no alternative but to comply. Undoing his coat, taking out his wallet, he removed all the Romanian Lei and handed them to the first man.

"And the rest?" the demand was also menacing.

"That's all I have." David added.

Meanwhile the second man was examining the notes in some detail. After a close scrutiny, he looked towards the first man and shook his head. Without a word, he passed the money back and, with a sweeping hand gesture, beckoned David to pass between the pair of them. David did not need any encouraging and, buttoning his coat, he swiftly walked the few yards to the embassy.

The Romanian soldier in his ill-fitting uniform hardly gave him a glance as he passed through the Embassy wrought iron gates into the Club building. Once inside he hung up his coat and felt the security and warmth not only of the building itself, but also of the company of George, who came over to greet him.

"Hello David. Good to see you. How's it going?"

David explained the incident with the guards and the money.

"The beggars!" It was the first time that David had seen George ruffled.

"They were in cahoots with the money-changer that you met round the corner from them. Most likely he had intended to give you marked Lei if you had been silly enough to get involved in his exchange. You did well not to be tempted."

David related the advice that his fellow passenger on the plane had given to him. "Good advice to have. Now tell me how have your negotiations gone so far."

David was delighted to have the opportunity to tell him of his successes on the Thursday and mentioned the presence of Mr Ilescu at the negotiation. George's expression changed.

"David, Ilescu is not their General Manager. He is from the Ministry of Security. Did he ask you any questions?"

David repeated the questions and answers that he had given.

George was silent for a few minutes. "We have had some feedback that the Ministry of Security is determined to find someone who they can pin the leaked industrial information on. Our information is that Ceauşescu has demanded a head and he doesn't care whose it is. Your questioning today means that you are being considered as a possible fall guy, but you are probably only one of many that they can put in the frame."

"Whew." David didn't know what other reaction to have to this information. "What do I do?"

"Just sit tight and don't get mixed up with anybody outside of this building until it all blows over. The way that they are going on, it won't be long before someone is in jail and it is much more likely to be someone who has been coming here regularly for some years. It's a good job that Harry is out of the country or he could easily have been set up."

David began to feel a little uncomfortable. If Harry had been the only one playing this dangerous game he would have certainly been a suspect. But, logically, David thought, they wouldn't suspect him as he had only arrived in Romania a week ago. Only a week ago? It seemed like a month. Dagenham and the North Circular road seemed a million miles away. For all its drabness the London suburbs now seemed a peaceful place to be. But he was here, and all that he could do was to follow George's advice and hope that the experience he had in the café in Piatuscu was not repeated.

He had it on the tip of his tongue to tell George about his trip too Brasov, but he held back, thinking that it might just raise other problems. Anyway, he was almost convinced that the incident was unconnected with the affair with the Minister..

"Hello David."

His thoughts were interrupted by Carol who appeared at George's elbow from nowhere. George was again relaxed and said that he hoped that the two of them would enjoy the film and that the first beer after the film was to be on him.

"Settling in to the Romanian scene?"

David took a fresh look at Carol. Slim, dark hair, very tidy but not too severely pulled back from a face that was attractive; her dark brown eyes looked straight at him.

"Hello. Er, yes I suppose so." He also noticed that the loose blouse was contoured gently over her nicely formed breasts.

"Anyway," went on Carol "Its Friday night so it's time to unwind. Are you going to see the film? It's a James Bond – *'From Russia with love'*. It's supposed to be good."

"Yes of course. Say, would you like a drink?"

"Yes I'd like that."

As they moved to the bar he was able to have a better view of his companion. As she walked in front of him he could see that she had a very trim figure. He pushed aside the thought that rushed to his head. This was not the Marina and was certainly not the place for a liaison. He ordered the drinks, they both chose beers; cheap at 10 Lei, about 40p. They settled at one of the tables at the side of the bar. David was conscious of the finishing touches going on at the end of the room – erecting the screen and putting out the chairs.

"What about you?" David asked Carol. "How do you cope?"

"Oh all right. Although it's more restrictive than other postings that I've been on because of the system."

"Where were you before?"

"Oslo, in Norway." Sorry, you know that, I mean you know that Oslo is in Norway. It is just that the country is always mentioned with posts." She looked even more attractive when she was flushed with embarrassment.

"Was that a good posting?"

"Oh yes. The landscape is so pretty, both in the summer and in the winter. And I learnt to ski."

"I tried once." David recounted his experience in Austria.

"Shame," said Carol "It is a pity that you didn't try Norway because their teaching system is better, at least I think so. And you can go ski walking, which is fun."

"What about the Norwegians? "David nearly added 'men' but stopped short.

"Oh they're pleasant enough but the men are a bit stubborn."

That expression caught David out. He wasn't sure what she meant. There was a call to take their seats for the film and they returned their glasses to the bar. To David's surprise, Carol linked her arm into his and escorted him to two chairs to the right of the seating. Uncoupling herself, she settled into the inner chair and the lights went down.

The film followed the usual James Bond theme: girls and more girls and dangerous situations where Bond nearly bought it, finally turning the tables on the bad guys. At one point in the film, where James Bond was cornered, David felt a hand clutch at his left leg. Carol had been caught up with the tension and instinctively grabbed him. Interestingly, she left her hand there for some time, catching David's eye and smiling before she slowly returned her hand to her lap.

David was beginning to feel stirrings that he hadn't felt since he'd left the UK. But he concentrated on the film in an effort to bring things back to near normal. The film finished with the usual blood and thunder, James Bond the hero, as always.

"Well that was good wasn't it? I always look forward to film nights, it brightens up the weekend. Now would you like a coffee?" Carol looked earnestly at him.

"Do they make real coffee here? I mean with Nescafe?" David had been brought up on 'Camp' coffee – the chicory flavoured liquid his mother used, or Nescafe.

"I do. I have some in my room. Would you like to come up?"

The sudden tightness in the chest that he always experienced on these occasions nearly caught him out but, steadying his voice, he answered that that would be very nice.

Carol took his hand and led him through a door on the right into a corridor with stairs going off. The architecture was very similar to the other building that he'd been in, high ornate ceiling and a balustraded shallow-stepped winding staircase.

They reached the next floor, and David was led to a pair of double doors. Carol pulled a key from the little pocket in her skirt, opened one door and stood aside for him to enter. The room was quite large, again with a high ceiling. In front of him was a French window and through the net curtain he could see protecting iron railings about waist high. The room was partly divided by a ceiling-high partition..

"Enter Chez Moi." The French was lost on him, but he guessed the meaning.

"Standard furniture for the foreign office." Carol extended her arm towards the modern furniture: two-seater settee and two fireside type chairs – they were similar to the ones David had bought his parents when his father was first ill, David thought.

"And through here," Carol led him to the opening in the partition, "the boudoir." David saw the bed and bedside table, bare chest of drawers and the austere wardrobe."

"And now for the coffee."

He hadn't noticed that there was another partitioned alcove in the bedroom area behind which was, he assumed, a water supply. Carol had disappeared and returned with an electric kettle, which she had plugged into the socket over the small table in the sitting room area.

"Sit yourself down." Carol indicated the settee.

"No television?"

"No, but then it's all Romania state programmes with a few Russian films thrown in. Ceauşescu doesn't allow the people to see the western world."

"Do you speak Romanian?"

"A little," Carol was continuing to prepare the coffee and had poured the boiling water into a filter pot, "but I speak French and Romanian is a Latin-based language, so one can make an educated guess at a lot of the words."

"I thought that German was spoken."

"More in the North – on the Hungarian border – a throw back to the Austro-Hungarian Empire."

The coffee was now ready and Carol brought the two mugs to the settee and sat down beside him. David sipped the coffee; it was a little too hot to drink. Carol had cupped her hands around her mug and sipped the contents. It was an attractive sight. There was a little pause and then Carol turned and put one hand on David's leg.

"And what about you?"

"What about me?" David was a little non-plussed by the chain of events.

"Well, have you found Bucharest interesting?"

"Interesting yes. But I certainly didn't expect some of the things that have happened."

David thought that he might venture a little further and lifted his arm to put it around Carol's shoulder. She pulled her hand up and slipped out of his arm.

"There is a time and a place for everything."

David's heart sank. He'd blown it. Putting her coffee down on the small table by the side of the settee she added, "Mind you perhaps this is the time and I know a place if you don't mind your coffee getting cold."

She took his coffee from him and put it with hers on the side table, pulled him gently up from the settee and led him to the bedroom area. Standing by the side of the three-quarter sized bed, Carol unbuttoned her blouse, untucking it from the waistband of her skirt and drew it off her shoulders. He had been right, she had nicely formed breasts.

"Well, do you want me to do it for you?" She came up to him and started to undo the top button of his shirt. "I'm sure you can manage the rest, you're a big boy now." She stepped back and continued to take off the rest of her attire.

David could hardly contain his excitement as he followed suit. He disrobed as fast as he could but Carol had already beaten him and was in bed with the sheets pulled up only to her waist. He slipped in beside her and then remembered that in his haste he had forgotten to remove his socks! As he struggled to reach down to take them, Carol asked him what was wrong.

"My socks, I forgot."

Carol caught his hand "I don't mind if you keep them on," and with that she lifted herself over him. David had considered himself to be a fairly experienced lover, but he recognised that here he was only a student and he was more than happy to let the mistress take over.

David used thoughts of all the all the worrying experiences that he had had since arriving in Romania, to prolong the lovemaking and put off the final moment. The climax, when it came, brought forth a harmony of ecstasy, as pleasurable to Carol as it was to him.

Lying back, this time with his arm around Carol, David quietly savoured the memory of what, for him, had been some of the best sex that he had ever had.

Some time later, Carol stirred. "David, are you going to be a regular to Bucharest?"

"I hope so." David was beginning to see some advantages in the regular visits.

"I'm not due to be re-posted until August next year so I will look forward to your visits," she hesitated, "if that's all right with you?"

All right with me? thought David. You bet your life it's all right with me.

"I'll look forward to that as well." Carol smiled.

"But in case either of us gets run over by a bus, let's live for today." Removing his arm, she pulled him, this time, on top of her.

When he awoke he had no idea what the time was. In the dim light from the sitting room he looked at his watch and saw that it was 12.40. His movement disturbed Carol, and she rose out of bed and quickly slipped on a cotton dressing gown.

"You'd better leave now, otherwise you'll draw the attention of the Romanian police. You can go straight out from the door at the bottom of the stairs. I'll show you."

Getting dressed took a little while: David's clothes had not been taken off in an orderly fashion. At least he didn't have to put his socks on! This would be a memory he'd savour! Leading him by the hand into the sitting room, Carol pulled him towards her for a last soft lingering kiss. Then she opened the doors and made sure that no one was around.

"Come again soon."

Gently pushing him out of the door she added, "the door in front of you, at the bottom of the stairs, will lead you out onto the front terrace. The gate is straight ahead. She gave him another brief kiss and turned back, leaving him to find his way down to the gate. The Romanian soldier stationed there gave him only a cursory glance. If only he knew, thought David, as he turned the corner to find his way back to the hotel.

Chapter 10

David was disturbed to find that he didn't wake up until 8.45; then he remembered that it was Saturday and he had no commitments for the day. He lay there for a little while savouring the memory of the night before. Perhaps the visits to Romania would not be so dull in the future.

He wondered how he could pass his time until the evening when he would again visit the Embassy Club. Who knows…?

Dressing slowly after his shower, he looked out of the balcony window on to the street below. Although there was little traffic, the battered buses still threw up the rancid smell of diesel exhaust, which was much more overpowering than that of the red buses back home. However, the day, although crisp, was bright and sunny.

Once down in the restaurant, he ordered hot water with a teabag and was served the usual slightly stale bread and butter with jam. He was surprised to notice how he had got used to this. What still annoyed him was the time that he had to wait before catching the attention of the waiters, and their indifference when they finally arrived.

He lingered a little, hoping that some company would come along, but now that Harry and Trevor had disappeared from the scene, apart from the few Germans in the hotel, there was little hope of finding someone to talk to.

After some time, David got up to go to the foyer where, at a desk, sat a Romanian tourist official. The man, about 45, looked up as he approached and, with a hand gesture, beckoned him to sit down.

"Good morning. Can I help you?"

"Well, perhaps you can. I was wondering what I could see of Bucharest. Is there anything that I should see whilst I am here?"

"Oh yes," the official, appeared to be pleased that he had a customer. "You should visit the Parcul Herăstrău."

Wait a minute, thought David; I've heard that name before. I know. That was the place that Mr Alexandru said was worth a visit – a park or something.

"The Parcul Herăstrău is one of our beautiful parks, but it is more than that," went on the official. "In the park we have assembled one of each of all the different old houses that existed in Romania, going back over a hundred years. They have been taken down piece by piece and re-assembled in the park. In some there are examples of the old household implements that we used in those days: bowls, cooking utensils, as well as some of the smallholding farm implements. Visitors can get some idea of what life was like in the past."

Did David sense some note of regret in his voice?

"I think that you will find it very interesting. And it is all free."

"'Sounds interesting. How do I get there?"

"You take the 47 bus which goes past the park."

"Where do I get the bus?"

"Just across the road." The official got up and led David to the glass windows at the front of the hotel. Drawing back the net curtain, he pointed to a bus stop sign. "There one of the bendy-buses."

David laughed. "One of the 'bendybuses', yes, the articulated ones."

"Wait a moment. I will write down the name of the park and you can hand it to the conductor so that she knows how much to charge you and when to tell you to get off."

The tourist official wrote on a slip of paper and handed it to David. "When you get back there is a theatre show in the beer garden just behind the hotel, a country dancing group are performing there this evening."

David thought that he would give this a miss. There might be other attractions more to his taste at the Club. Thanking the official, David made his way outside and crossed the wide street to the bus stop where a number of people were waiting. Two buses came along and people got on and off. Then the 47 bus arrived. It proved to be a rather more battered noisy articulated bus than he'd seen before with a concertina joining centre piece.

The door opened and he was swept inside by the group that had collected whilst he was waiting. He only managed to get just inside because of the number of passengers already on board. Once inside he was forced to stand nose to nose with the other passengers, almost unable to move his arms. Suddenly, he was aware that he was the centre of attention. The man next to him poked him in the ribs and jerked his hand towards the far end of the bus. David diverted his eyes in that direction and became aware of a woman in a navy jacket sitting in an elevated seat waving to him and rubbing her fingers.

He realised that this must be the conductor and that she was asking for his fare. But how much? Digging in this pocket he pulled out a 10 Lei coin. He also got out the note that the tourist official had written for him. He held these up and they were taken by the 'nose to nose' fellow passenger. They were passed hand to hand by various passengers to the conductor. She looked at the note, pulled some change from the leather bag hanging around her neck, produced a ticket from somewhere and then, with a reverse operation, the note plus some coins and the ticket were returned to him. It was too cramped to check the change there and then, but he later found that the journey had only cost one and a half Lei.

The bus rumbled on and, although it was very hot, there was surprisingly no body odour from those around him. After about 20 minutes, David noticed that there were fewer and fewer buildings beside the road. He felt a nudge to his arm and his attention was directed to the conductor who was waving furiously to him as the bus stopped. The people close to him moved aside to allow him to get to the door. Assuming that this was what he was meant to do, he eased himself through the bodies and got off the bus. He stood for a moment and watched the bus rumble noisily on its way. Looking around he saw that he was at the entrance to the park and a few yards to his right were the heavy wrought iron gates that formed an entrance through the railings that surrounded the park.

Once inside the gate, he followed the path and after a short distance saw the first of the re-assembled houses. This was a type of bungalow, made of wood with a shallow overhanging roof. It was obviously very old; the wood was twisted and aged. He went up to it and, once inside, he found two rooms. One was obviously where the family slept with cupboard type beds set in the wall. The other was a communal room with a table in the centre on which there were black iron heavy pans and other implements. It was quite a strange sensation to know that he was standing in the home that someone lived in over 100 years ago.

David noticed a small party of children being led into the next house. They were being directed by a woman of about 50, who was instructing the children in a lesson, as they moved in and out of the houses. There was also a fresh-faced young man of about the same age as David keeping up the rearguard.

As they moved on, so did David. The next house was similar to the first but slightly different in the layout. There were agricultural implement hanging on one wall. If anything, this house looked older than the first. On emerging from the house, he noticed a leather-jacketed man who looked vaguely familiar. After some moments' thought he recognised him as one of the passenger on the 'bendy' bus. As he looked back at him, the man, who had been watching David, quickly turned his eyes away. David wondered if he was getting paranoid or if he was really being followed. He put the idea aside and decided to proceed to the next exhibit. He had hardly stepped out of the building when he thought he saw the fresh-faced young man who had been with the children, moving towards him. 'Leather jacket' was still only about 30 yards away looking intently at some farm implements on show. David carried on towards the next house, which, although slightly different on the outside from the first one, had similar furnishings.

Coming out of the house he was suddenly confronted by the young man that he had seen at the rear of the children's party.

"Are you English?" The voice was obviously foreign. The man looked as if he was a local.

"Yes?" David's response had an inquiring tone.

"Do they know about the children?" The young man's voice was now more animated.

"I'm sorry 'the children'? I'm not with you."

"They must know about the children. They must do something about it." The man was becoming increasingly disturbed.

David's puzzlement was increasing; suddenly he felt a searing pain in his head and the world plunged into darkness.

Chapter 11

David's recollection was blurred, but after a few minutes he realised that he was in the back of a car with the leather-jacketed man sitting next to him. He had the impression that the car was moving at quite a speed but he had no idea in what direction. He tried to raise his hand to soothe his aching head but found that he couldn't move it. Looking down, he found the cause. He was handcuffed to our leather-jacketed friend.

"What's going on?" David's voice was weak.

There was no answer, so he repeated the question. His handcuffed companion said some words, supposedly in Romanian, to the driver who, without turning his head, answered the question in stilted English.

"You will see when we get to the bureau."

The bureau? What the hell was he talking about? Before David could press for an explanation, the car came to a halt and, still handcuffed, he was pulled out roughly. He found himself in front of a large building, again ornate in style, the entrance of which was guarded by two soldiers placed at the bottom of the five steps leading up to a large heavy door.

The door opened as he reached the top step and he was half dragged along a corridor to an open doorway to the left. As he was led inside he noticed that there were no windows, or if they were, they had been blacked out. The lighting was quite dim.

'Leather jacket' then pushed David towards a chair. This was one of the two chairs in the room, the only furniture besides a table. The handcuffs were removed by L.J.

"May I ask what the hell is going on?" David felt that it was time to assert himself. There was no response. Then, through the doorway, closing the door after him, came a second man. He was rather heavily built, balding and dressed in a blue uniform with some gold insets in the epaulets of his jacket. For a time he just stood looking at David. Then, drawing up the chair on the other side of the table, he spoke in a clipped voice.

"You are Mr David Edwards?"

"Yes but..."

"You are here to visit our enterprises?"

"Yes, I'm discussing contracts with two enterprises."

"Then why do you make arrangements to meet with subversive people of the Romanian Republic"? His voiced was raised now.

"I'm sorry...?"David was completely at sea.

"You make arrangements to meet your contact in the park, where you hope that you will not be noticed. That was silly of you." The man's voice was raised even further and his posture at the table took on a threatening stance.

"I didn't make any arrangements to meet anybody," David managed to stammer out. "I went to the park to see the old houses. Who am I supposed to have made arrangements with?"

The question was ignored. "Who are you working for?"

"K.M Industrial."

"We know that is the reason you have been giving for your visit to Romania. What is the organisation behind your planned meetings?"

"I'm sorry I don't know what the hell you are talking about. I went to the park to see the buildings."

Then the penny dropped. The 'subversive person' was the fresh-faced young man who had approached him. The children! Should he mention the children? Thinking quickly, he thought that the least they thought that he knew, the better.

"Look. If it's anything to do with that chap talking to me, I don't know who he was or what he was saying. He had a strong accent. He could have been saying something in English but I couldn't understand him."

David looked at the inquisitor who now appeared to be a little less aggressive.

"We shall have to wait until we have made further enquiries. We are dealing with your contact. You will come with us."

"But I don't have a contact. As I said, I went to the park to see the houses." This seemed to fall upon deaf ears. Before he could react further, L.J had snapped the handcuffs on him again and he was pulled from the chair and led along the corridor until they reached some stairs leading downwards. At the bottom of a short flight he was lead into another room, this time it was fitted out only with a bunk. Again it was dimly lit. The handcuffs were taken off and his captors left before he could protest, slamming the door shut behind them.

Bewildered by the rapid events, David sat on the bunk, trying desperately to decide what his next action should be. In films he had seen people in similar situations demand to see their consulate, but how could he do that now, isolated in this cell-like room.

Resigned that he could do nothing about his predicament, he stretched out on the bunk to try to relieve his headache. The tenderness and swelling at a point just at the back of his head confirmed that he had been hit hard on the head by 'a blunt instrument' A police truncheon? Perhaps it was the reaction to the blow, or nature's way of relieving the pain, but he found himself drifting into a disturbed sleep. He dreamed that he was being lead away by some children to see something, but before he could see what it was, everything became totally black.

David was awoken by the noise of the door being unlocked, followed by the entry of two uniformed men. Neither of these men had anything on their epaulets. Reaching down, they lifted him from the bunk and frog-marched him out of the room and up the stairs to the same room that he had been taken to before.

The epaulet-decorated character was there but also present, to his utter relief, was George from the Embassy.

"George!"

Before David could say any more. George intervened.

Turning to the official he said, "I can see that Mr Edwards has been well looked after. Now, as you accept that he is innocent of any charges you brought against him, may I suggest that we close the matter?"

There was no reply but after a short pause there was a short nod of assent.

"Come on David. We'll go and have a drink at the club shall we?" With that George took a firm hold of David's arm and wheeled him round and out of the room. Once outside George said in almost a whisper, "Say nothing."

The embassy car was waiting outside and they both got in the back. Still George said nothing and David, obeying orders, kept quiet. The car entered the embassy grounds and George helped David get out – he was still a little unsteady on his feet. As George instructed the driver to return the car to the parking lot, he beckoned David to lead the way to the club doorway.

Once inside, David was helped to a comfy seat in the lounge area by the mature lady member of the embassy who had initially welcomed him into the club. George who had momentarily disappeared, reappeared beside David with two glasses of what he soon found out was whiskey. Although this was not his favourite tipple, he gladly took it and sank the glass in almost one gulp. Contrary to his expectation, it was a pleasant experience.

"George..." He was determined to find out what had happened and what it was all about.

"Sit quietly for a moment old chap. I will try to explain what I believe is the background to this." David waited for him to begin.

"Starting at the beginning, it appears that you were followed from the time you left the hotel. The reason for this, I believe, is that they still have a bee in their bonnet about Harry and his sudden disappearance. They have suspicions of a connection with the case against Golescu, the Minister. You remember he was shot because he was found to be giving advance information on pending contracts to Western companies." David realised that he had been right not to mention the handwritten paper or that he had destroyed it.

"But I couldn't have had anything to do with that." David protested.

"They need a fall guy to satisfy Ceauşescu. And the fact that you are with the same agency is good enough to put you in the frame." George paused whilst he lit a cigarette. Half apologetically he re-opened the packet and offered David one. David shook his head. He'd given up smoking some years back.

"Then when the dissident came up to you, which, I believe, was purely by chance, our tailing friend was on hand to call for assistance to prevent you getting too much information. By the way, did you tell the security people what he had said?"

"No"

"Good for you. If they thought that he had passed information over to you, they may have kept you longer."

"But how did you know that I had been picked up?" David showed some of the relief that he felt in the question.

"Luckily, a friend of the dissident saw what had happened and telephoned the embassy. The call was anonymous of course, but it helped us trace where you had been taken. I was able to convince them that you had been advised to visit the park by Mr Dieter and that you had no part in any pre-arranged meeting. Also, that you were just about to call the police to deal with the young man when you were picked up".

"Picked up! I was slugged and I've got the bump to prove it." David could still feel the bump, although his headache was easing.

"What did he mean when he asked me if we knew about the children?"

Looking a little embarrassed, George went on. "You don't know how clever you were saying nothing. That is a really sensitive subject. What this young man was trying to do was to bring attention to a situation that we, in the Western world, know all about but can do nothing to rectify. You see, for various reasons, partly because of the persecution of the gypsies, there are a number of orphaned children in Romania. Ceauşescu has decided that out of sight out of mind is the best policy with regard to these and he has removed them to isolated homes. The conditions under which the children exist are horrific, some apparently never leaving their cots. Consequently there is a lot of disease and many deaths.

Your young man was one of the few who are brave enough to want to do something about the situation, but he is, or was, wasting his time. Any approach to the Romanian government would result in a denial that these existed and the Western world cannot risk a confrontation with the Soviet Union who, in spite of their misgivings on Ceauşescu, would rush to his side".

"So we do nothing?"

"That's politics for you David," George smiled wryly.

"And what will happen to the young man?"

"He will not see the light of day for some time, if ever."

"Can we do nothing about his situation?"

"Again there is no mileage in that for the British or other Western governments."

"It doesn't seem right" David felt helpless.

"That's politics." George repeated.

"But this young man must believe that he can do something or he wouldn't have taken the risk of contacting me."

"David, there are always people who will fight for a cause. But in our case there is little we can do about it without creating a diplomatic incident, which in the short term has little chance of success and would prejudice many other issues."

In his present state all this was too much for David to take in. Perhaps when he was fitter he could again broach the subject. In the meantime the whiskey was beginning to work and sooth his emotions a little. David felt that it was time to leave. He looked at his watch and saw that it was almost 5.p.m. He had arrived at the park shortly after 10.a.m., so he calculated that he must have been unconscious for some time.

"I think that I'll go back to the hotel and have a shower. Is the club open tonight?"

"Yes but the film is the same as last night."

Last night. The memory started to excite him. "Is Carol off duty this evening?"

"Oh I forgot to tell you." George looked a little embarrassed, but why this should be, David didn't know. "Carol has gone back to base for a few days. Our courier went sick and it was important that the diplomatic bag got back; she won the draw to take it and will return on Tuesday. A few days away from here is very welcome from time to time."

Initially a feeling a deep disappointment came over David. Then remembering how fit he needed to be to keep up with Carol, he decided that he would rather be on top form when invited to take up the opportunity again. Next time, he smiled to himself, he would remember to take off his socks.

David bade his leave and walked the short distance to the hotel where, having collected his key, he made his way via the lift to his penthouse suite. Once there, he slipped off his trousers and shirt and lay on the bed intending to doze for about an hour before showering and going down to eat. The doze lasted a little more than an hour. The subsequent meal was as uninteresting as it had been all week: two pork chops and some salad and soggy chips, but at least it kept body and soul together.

After the meal he strolled up to the Embassy Club where, as he wasn't able to see Carol, he spent an hour or so with Siggie, the German, who was a fount of amusing stories connected with his sausage skin buying expeditions in Eastern Europe and Outer Mongolia. In Outer Mongolia, according to Siggie, his car ended up loaded with an excess of tins of meat and other things he traded; he didn't dare to eat any of the Mongolian preparations.

He also related a few of his sexual exploits, which made David laugh. There was no doubt though, Siggie was a character and he kept David amused for the whole of the evening. Feeling a little tired after the long day, David left the Club; the short walk back to the hotel in the cool air didn't revive him. Collecting his key from the reception desk, David made his way up to his penthouse suite; now convinced that he deserved the so-called extra luxury of the penthouse.

Leaving the lift, David put his key in the lock only to find that the door was already unlocked. Pushing open the door, he found himself suddenly thrown back into the carpeted hallway.

Chapter 12

Confused but unhurt David turned his head, just enough to see someone running down the corridor to the stairway. He eased himself up, but realised that there was no point in trying to follow the fleeing man. Instead he stepped into his suite. He could see in the fully lit room that his briefcase had been opened and all the catalogues and papers had been taken out and were now strewn everywhere. The wardrobe was open and, from the disorder of his clothing, it was obvious that this had also been ransacked.

David's mind flew back to the handwritten slip of paper that he had found in Harry's catalogue. He was thankful now that he had disposed of it at the first opportunity.

He tried to collect his thoughts and understand who and what was behind the intrusion. It could be someone trying to implicate him in the Golescu affair or, alternatively, it could be someone who had been receiving favours from Harry and was frightened that David could be in possession – as in fact he had been – of something that could incriminate them.

David felt that it would be pointless to complain to the hotel manager about the intrusion and decided that some good could have come out the incident, as the intruder had found nothing, probably convincing him that David at least, was 'clean'.

A wave of tiredness came over him and, tidying up the papers, David decided that apart from putting a chair against the door when he went to bed, there was little more that he could do.

Climbing into bed, he was asleep within minutes.

Sunday passed off uneventfully. After the experiences of the previous day, David decided not to do any more exploring and stayed in bed until well after 9 o'clock. He ambled down for a late breakfast-cum-lunch and spent the rest of the day reading, breaking off only to visit the Corinthian Palace Hotel, where he took a beer in the conservatory.

While he was sitting there he was approached by man who, by his appearance, was obviously a Westerner. He had an American accent and introduced himself as Pete. Seating himself he immediately began, like most Americans that David had met, to talk all about himself and his interests.

It appeared that he bought, like the passenger on the plane, Romanian national costume clothing for sale in his New York store. In spite of being an American and a New Yorker, he was rather quiet and fairly sophisticated. The afternoon developed and Pete became chummier, finally suggesting that they met up later for dinner in the cabaret room. David, with no Carol to meet, agreed. They were presented with the same dull meal as they would have been served in the restaurant. The cabaret, although the same act that he had watched on his previous visit with Harry, was still entertaining. The Romanian folk dancers were good and again the whiff of body odour still drifted across the room after they finished the frantic dance routine.

"That's the stuff I buy," said Pete, pointing to the costumes. "Goes down like a bomb in the village y'know?" David suspected that he was talking about Greenwich Village and nodded. The show finished and David felt he ought to get to bed as he had an early start the following day – Monday. As he bade Pete a goodnight, Pete also got to his feet.

"Say what about a night cap in my room before you turn in? I've got a bottle of really old Scotch I brought in."

David was tempted but saying that this time he would give it a miss but agreeing that they must do it again sometime, he retired for the night. There was an almost imperceptible change to Pete's expression, but then the smile was back again.

"Well, suit yourself. Anyway, have a good trip tomorrow. At least you won't be worried about the traffic." With that he turned and left the bar.

Wait a minute. David was confused. How did he know that he was going on a trip? And the mention of traffic meant that he must have known that he was travelling somewhere by car.

David recalled the exchanges between them. Pete had been full of himself but, with normal English reticence, David had held back any information about his business. He certainly didn't mention any trip.

David looked at his watch, just after 10.00 p.m. Would the club still be open? David felt a sudden urgent need to talk to George. Without waiting to go back to his room for his coat, David hurried out into the chill night air and down the main street to the turning for the Embassy. The lights were still on and the door still attended. Once inside he spotted George who was in conversation with a Swedish looking chap who he had not seen before.

"George, Can I grab you for a minute?"

"Hello David, I didn't think we would see you here tonight." His relaxed manner was comforting. David described his meeting with the American. Listening carefully, George's face clouded. "American accent, you say?"

"Yes he said that he was from New York. I can't tell you if it was a New York accent, but he was quieter than I would have expected."

"And you definitely didn't give him any idea of your plans?"

"Definitely not."

George paused, looking a little thoughtful.

"David. This is serious. We have just received in the courier bag, notification of a so-called American who is collaborating with the Romanians. They warned us in case he tried to come into the club. I suspect this is another way to get you, I mean your company, to confess to an involvement with the bribing of the Minister. They must have convinced themselves that Harry was involved – and with his sudden disappearance, I can understand why." David felt that it was better not to tell him of the handwritten piece of paper and the intruder. "You did well not to go back to his room with him; it is most likely to be bugged."

David was feeling worried, but George relaxed a little. "Not to worry, now you're on your guard they are not going to compromise you. Just carry on as normal but, as mother used to say, don't talk to strangers. Now what about that Scotch? We also have some very old stuff."

Putting his arm around his shoulder, he steered David to the bar in the corner of the lounge and very quickly David found a large glass of the hard stuff in his hand. After finishing this, and with the buzz of easy conversation around him, David felt better. Remembering that he had an early start, he excused himself and hurried back to the hotel and to his room. Feeling more secure, he was quickly in bed and, helped by the Scotch, was soon fast asleep.

Chapter 13

When he woke it was dark. Looking at his watch he was astounded to see that it was 5.30 a.m., he hadn't stirred all night. He lay quietly for a little while, falling in and out of sleep, until the next time he looked at his watch it showed 6.00.a.m. He suddenly remembered that he had to travel to Resita. Washing and dressing in a rush, he went down to the snack bar, managed to persuade the barman to serve a cup of coffee in reasonably quick time and hurried to the garage to collect the 1800.

Although he had all day to travel to the Hotel in Resita, he didn't want to reach the town in the dark. The route took him back over part of the same journey that he had made on the Friday, but this time he decide not to stop in Piatescu. On passing the square his breathing became a little faster but it slowed down once he was out in the countryside again. He was only a few miles out when the hurried departure from the hotel caught up with him. The coffee, without anything else to soak it up, suddenly made a 'natural break' necessary.

Although there was little activity on the road, his natural instinct was to find somewhere private. Seeing a small track on the right, he pulled in and stopped the car. He got out, only just in time judging by the pressure building in his bladder, and moved towards the bushes.

The lengthy discharge gave him time to look around. The area was typical of the areas that he had already seen: large fields, with some sunflowers in a field some little way to the left. However to the right, further up the track, he noticed quite a large ornate building standing on its own. Could this be the orphanage? 'Sensitive' and 'Caught trying to break in.' The words of Deutmann were still familiar in his ears.

His common sense told him that he shouldn't stray off the path, but his natural curiosity convinced him that if he made a normal approach he couldn't get into trouble. He couldn't help remembering the anguish on the face of the young man in the park. Leaving his car he followed the path, which lead up to the building. He finally reached a large door in the middle of what appeared to be a very large house, although he noticed that there were no curtains at any of the windows.

Opening the door, he entered a spacious hall with a high ceiling and a winding balustrade staircase leading off to the left. The first thing that struck him was the smell. The stench was overpowering. He thought that it was predominately urine mixed with other equally unpleasant body odours. Almost immediately a door on the right opened and a woman of about 40 years of age came out. She stopped in her tracks as she saw him. The Romanian, she addressed him in Romanian, appeared agitated.

"Sorry?"

This seemed to increase her agitation. Rushing towards him, she almost dragged him through the doorway into the room from which she had just appeared. She closed the door behind her and stood for a moment with her back against it almost as if she were trying to hold it from a possible assault from the outside. David looked round and found that he was in a room filled with children's cots. The stench was as strong as ever but there was an even stranger phenomenon. None of the small children in the cots was making a sound.

"You are English?"

David nodded.

"What are you doing here? Don't you know that you cannot come in here?"

"But surely you have visitors here from time to time?"

"Never. It is not allowed."

"But the children, what is wrong with them?"

Without waiting for him to answer, she herded him through another small door into a smaller room with a table and two chairs.

"You must not stay here. How did you get here?"

He explained that he was on his way to Resita and stopped 'for a short break from the driving' and saw the house. The woman started to pace the room. "You must go before anyone sees you. Wait here." With that she left the room.

David, realising for the first time that he may have bitten off more than he could chew, stood motionless – not even daring to sit down. There was still no sound coming from the children. The stench was even more penetrating. After what appeared to be some considerable time, the woman returned.

"Quick, come." David followed her out of the room; she turned left out of the doorway, not right towards the main door that he had come in through. She led him to a smaller door and beckoned him towards her. Opening the door she said, "There is a small track outside that is bordered by bushes. Take that and it will lead you on to the path you came up, quite near the road. Please, please hurry and do not tell anyone that you have been here." With that she almost pushed him through the door, which she then immediately slammed closed.

David hurried down the path, pleased to find that he was shielded from view on both sides by the bushes. True to her word, the track came out on the original path that he had taken and close to where he had parked the 1800. He got in and started the engine and was away almost before he had shut the door. Back on the road he began to relax. But could not get the awful smell and the unnatural silence of the children lying in their cots out of his mind. Why didn't they show any interest when he was in the room? Children have a natural curiosity, but most of them just lay there.

As the journey continued he pondered over his experiences since he had arrived in Romania, none were pleasant, except the very pleasant evening spent with Carol. Then he remembered the incident with the young man in the park and the description of the homes that George had described. When George had told him about the situation he really hadn't taken it in. Now having experienced the silence of all those children, coupled with the smell, it came home to him what terrible conditions these poor children were living in.

It seemed incredible that nothing was being done about it. For the first time he realised how naive he was about worldly matters. Cosseted by the general even-handedness and openness that existed back home in England, it had never crossed his mind to consider that such conditions did not prevail worldwide. David also recalled the probable fate of the young man in the park and wondered how close he had come to being in a similar situation if he had been caught in the house.

He reflected that in the short time he had been in Romania he had been caught up in some scary situations. Perhaps in later years he would be able to get a pint or two from an interested audience relating his experiences, but were they worth it? For now he was here, there was a job to do and he intended to do it to the best of his ability. Very successfully, in fact. He began to relish again how successfully he had carried out the negotiations; it helped pass the time on the long journey to Resita.

At about 1:30 he passed the sign for Resita. He was just wondering how he would find the Loco Works when he passed a large factory. A little further on there was a large entrance with the sign 'LOCOMOTIV WERKE' on the iron gates that stood open. He drove into the large yard and noticed piles of steel bars and plate on his left whilst on the right there were semi-assembled railway axles. Further on there was a three-storey brick building that obviously housed the offices. From the look of the bricks, the building had been around for some years.

David parked the car and as he got out he noticed a strong burning smell. It was familiar. It was the same smell that he had smelled for the two years he had worked at Ford Motor works in Dagenham when he was a draughtsman and had his drawing board in an office close to the foundry. The smell was from the casting shop where molten metal was poured into the moulds filled with resin-bonded sand. They were obviously producing their own casting here.

Parking his car next to the single Dacia parked in front of the building, David got out and strode up to the building, entering through the large double doors. Inside was a reception hall with a reception window on one side. This was unmanned, but a bell push alongside the window invited pressing. The ring produced a middle aged dark skinned man who looked up enquiringly at David.

"I have an appointment with Mr Dinicu Mihail."

Without a word, the man turned and left the reception office. David used the time to explore the reception hall. Cream and brown, as usual, but this time there were two pictures. One was of a large diesel locomotive and the other of a group of men standing in front of what could have been the front of this building. Looking at it he had seen similar photos in England in some the showrooms or reception areas of his customers. Maybe it was a works outing. At this moment the door at the rear of the reception area opened and a mature grey haired man made his way towards him.

"Mr Edwards." It was not a question but a welcoming statement made with an open smile. "Please come in." Mr Mihail, he presumed. David followed him through the door and arrived in an office with a large old-fashioned desk and a mahogany conference table with ornate legs. At least the place had some style, unlike the offices in Bucharest with their melamine furniture.

"Please sit down." Mihail beckoned him to a leather-seated chair by the table. "It is nice of you to come." David was impressed with his lack of accent. "But please first of all, will you take a coffee? Or would you prefer tea?"

Tea, the first time he had been offered tea. Before he could answer this Mr Mihail said, "I am afraid it will be a tea bag in hot water not 'tea like mother used to make'." He smiled.

"Tea please. That would be very nice." Mihail lifted the telephone and said a few words then, replacing the telephone, looked across at David, smiling.

"How was the journey? Not too bad I hope."

"No," David had decided not to mention the diversion, but at some time, he thought to himself, he had to find out why the children in the cots were not making a noise. "There is a lot less traffic here than in England."

Again Mihail smiled, "Yes, we don't have many cars but they say it will get better soon." He sounded a little sceptical with this last remark.

"Mr Mihail, you speak very good English. How did you come to speak it so well?"

"When I first joined the Resita Locomotive Co. – that was its name before the war – I was sent to Swindon in England, to the Great Western Railway yard and stayed there for about 6 months. It was a nice period for me. The people were very nice and they helped me to improve the English that I had learnt in school and college. Unfortunately I don't now get a chance to practise it and the only reading I can do is the technical manuals."

Before the war! He must be in his 60s David thought.

"So the works is very old then?"

"Yes it was founded just about the turn of the century. I joined the company from college at 18, that is over 45 years ago." He had a twinkle in his eye now.

"You have seen some changes then?" Oh my God David thought, I've made a political remark – fool.

"Yes, things are different now. We were more bound together." David recalled the picture in the reception hall of the group of men standing in front of the building. Very definitely a works outing, he thought.

"And there was more dedication." Mihail looked a little nostalgic then, brightening up, went on, "Still we can't do anything about that now."

David had a thought. "Would you mind if I go out to my car for a minute?"

"Of course not." Mihail looked a little puzzled.

David retraced his steps and, unlocking the 1800, pulled his canvas overnight bag out of the back seat. Zipping it open, he got out his Neville Shute paperback *A Town like Alice*. Returning to the office, he placed the paperback on the table.

"Perhaps you would like to have this, I have finished with it." A little white lie but it didn't matter.

"That is very kind of you," Mihail looked a little embarrassed, "I will enjoy that."

"Tell me," he went on "you find things a little different here in Romania, I mean different to England? He saw David hesitate.

"Oh you shouldn't mind me. I am not one of them." David couldn't quite bring himself to disclose his thoughts but before he could say anything Mihail continued.

"There are many things that are wrong in Romania. Ceauşescu wants to cover up the truth too much." Then, rather defiantly, "I am only tolerated because the rest of the management here cannot think for themselves and they know that I can make up for their inefficiencies."

David was beginning to believe that there was at least one Romanian who was not tainted with the Communist brush.

"I agree about the inefficiencies," David nodded cautiously, "and officials seem to be very heavy handed at times." He related the incident at Piatuscu.

Mihail listened carefully. Then said, "That is because you were not far from one of the orphanages."

"Orphanages?" David thought that he ought at this point to appear naive about the situation.

"Ceauşescu decided that orphans and mentally retarded children should be isolated from outsiders. It is all part of hiding the truth. Some of the orphans have resulted from the actions taken by Ceauşescu. There is one of the orphanages just outside of Piatuscu."

David started to feel a little perspiration appear on his forehead.

"Is that the big building on the right just a little way out on the way to Bucharest from here?"

"You saw it?"

"I not only saw it, I went inside it." He explained the circumstances.

Mihail again listened intently.

"You have been very kind," he said pointing to the book. "You must now promise me something, in fact two things." David nodded.

"Firstly that you will not tell this experience to any one else in Romania. What you did was very dangerous." David nodded again.

"And secondly, you will never admit to anyone that you have spoken to me about it. Even though I am too old to care about what they do to me, I still value my freedom enough not to tempt fate. I would be placed in a very difficult position because under the law anything you tell me that is not to do with our business I have to report to the police within 24 hours."

Was he stupid to tell him all this, David thought and, almost reading his mind, Mihail continued.

"Do not worry. It is not my habit to conform but it is still a serious matter. You promise?"

"Yes. Of course."

As he spoke the man from the reception area arrived with a Turkish coffee, a cup with the tea bag and a small jug of milk. From the look of it, the milk was probably sterilised. His mother used to buy that when he was a boy before fridges came to be the norm. Mihail turned to the man as if the past conversation hadn't happened.

"Ah good our tea and coffee has arrived. I am afraid we do not know how to make English tea but the tea bag is the next best thing."

At that point the door opened again and a young pleasant-looking man entered, holding the door open for the drinks waiter as he left.

"Ah! Meet Dimitru Bogdan, my assistant." Mr Bogdan came forward and shook David's hand firmly. "How do you do." The phrase was obviously a practised one. David just nodded in acknowledgement.

"Bogdan doesn't speak much English but can understand quite a lot, so if you will speak slowly we can start." Mr Bogdan drew up the chair that was indicated by Mihail, who had already slipped the Neville Shute book into his drawer.

David opened his briefcase and took out his catalogues and proceeded to explain about his products. He felt pleased and relaxed that he could now get back on to familiar safe ground. After a further hour or so of discussion, during which Mihail translated one or two areas of detail to Mr Bogdan, they came to the end of their talks.

David started to pack his brochures into his briefcase. Mihail got up and nodded to Bogdan who rose and extended his hand to David. "It was nice meeting you." Again a practised phrase, he thought. David nodded and said, "And you," which was obviously the cue for to the young man to leave.

"He is a nice young man," Mihail commented. "In different times he could go far. Now you are stopping at the Hotel Comercial, I believe? You will find it about 2 kilometres further down on the road you came in, just as you get to the town centre and the square. Thank you for coming and remember your promise." David nodded vigorously.

Hurrying to the 1800. David reflected that this was the first time that he had met a Romanian who was, in a guarded way, prepared to indicate that all was not well. Perhaps it was because of his age –according to what he said he was 63 years old and a little cavalier with his future. However, there was no doubt that he had scared David, causing a slight tightening in his stomach when he realised what the consequences of being caught in the orphanage could have been. Still, he couldn't get out of his mind the awful smell and the unaccountable silence of so many young bodies.

David drove out through the large iron gates and turned left into the town. Sure enough, the Hotel was on the left, standing back a little from the road, a concrete rendered building with a gunmetal coloured aluminium and glass door at the top of a few entrance steps. Grabbing his overnight bag, he entered to find the reception desk of light oak immediately in front of him, with a tallish thin man in a grey cotton-type jacket standing behind it. He tried to smile, but his recent experience made it difficult.

"David Edwards. I have a room reserved here."

The man looked down at a book on the top of the counter and nodded.

"Passport please."

David's heart stopped. He pictured his passport in the bottom drawer of the bedside table in his room at the Theodore; he had tucked it there for safety before retiring for the night.

"I'm afraid that I left it in Bucharest – at the Hotel."

"You cannot stop here without your passport." The man had shut the book as if he wanted to demonstrate the finality of his statement.

"I can get someone to go and get it and telephone you with the details." Someone from the Embassy could go and pick it up, he thought.

"You cannot stay here without your passport." He repeated the statement with his hands resting firmly over the closed register.

"But I have no way of getting back tonight."

It was almost as if the man was programmed; all he did was repeat his statement. Realising there was an impasse, David had no alternative but to pick up his bag and return to the car. It was getting dark outside, but there was nothing he could do but to plough his way back to Bucharest, all of 5 hours, and in the dark too. Perhaps he could pull in on the way and take a nap in the car. He had his overcoat, thank goodness, and that could give him some warmth.

Once back inside the 1800, he turned the car to the left for the journey back. He passed the iron gates of the locomotive works and was surprised how quickly darkness was falling.

In the headlights he could make out the straight road out of the town. At least he wouldn't have to worry about any traffic, even the odd tractor he had seen on the way had turned in for the night. He realised that his main problems was keeping alert. There were no 'cats eyes' to give him warning of bends ahead. Settling down, he concentrated on keeping his eyes on the beam of light in front of him.

Some time passed and he estimated that he must be coming close to the area where the orphanage was situated. He certainly wasn't going to stop anywhere near there. He would give a good half an hour's distance between him and the building before pulling over to take a short nap.

Afterwards he thought that he should have noticed them, but he didn't see the two wide tracks of mud across the road. The tracks led out of a field and were obviously the deposits from one of the large tractors he had seen earlier.

The next thing he knew was that the 1800 was travelling, crab like, across the road and there was nothing he could do to bring it back into a straight line. Then everything went black.

Chapter 14

There was some faint recollection of hands pulling at him, but when full consciousness came he found himself in a bed, a big bed with a thick down mattress in which he had sunk. He hadn't experienced that sort of mattress since he was a young boy when they were on all the beds in his mother's house. He'd thrown them out when his father became ill and replaced them with spring mattresses, not that they were any more comfortable. In fact they were not as warm in the winter.

The other recollection was the stinking headache that throbbed when he tried to move his head. Move it he did though, curious to explore his surrounding in the dim light. It was a large room with a small window. It was low-ceilinged and, as far as he could see, had little furniture except for a padded chair, a big wardrobe and a table on which was standing a large bowl. At that moment, a door in the corner, which he hadn't yet noticed, opened and a woman of about fifty entered. She had a bowl of something in her hands. Following her was a younger woman; David guessed that she was in her twenties. It was the younger woman who spoke.

"You are better?" Her English was accented but very clear. The older lady had put her arm under David's head and was trying to lift him up. The headache was excruciating but he tried to give her some assistance in pulling himself up to a more upright position.

"My head hurts."

"Yes, you bumped your head against the glass. Please try to let my mother give you the soup. It has some herbs in it which may help your head."

He had no option. The mother was attempting to pour the soup into his mouth, which she forced open with the thick rim of the bowl. It was hot, a bit spicy but not bad. She paused for a little while whilst David swallowed a full mouthful then repeated the procedure. The younger woman stood by, watching. The whole process took about ten minutes as David had to drink the soup a mouthful at a time. When the bowl was empty a cloth was produced and the older lady proceeded to clean up the inevitable dribbles round his chin. David slid back into a prone position. The younger one, slim and dark with nearly black hair, still stood looking down at him.

"What happened?" His enquiry was addressed to the younger one.

"Your vehicle"(vehicle, not car he noticed) "slided off the road into the ditch. You hit your head and were not awake when my father found you."

"Where am I?"

"You are in our house. We will look after you until you can drive again."

"How is the car?"

"My father will make it OK when you can go."

"But I mean where am I? How far am I from Bucharest?"

"You are in the village of Bros. We about 5 km from Piatuscu."

Piatuscu! It must be fate thought David.

"But now you must sleep." She came close and tucked the heavy eiderdown round his shoulders and then, with a smile, backed towards the door finally turning to disappear. Whether it was the soup, or whether he was still suffering from concussion he couldn't tell, but his eyelids drooped and he was soon fast asleep.

When he awoke it was quite dark. His headache was almost gone and all he could feel was a little bruising on his right side. He was trying to piece together what had happened. He could remember seeing the mud tracks. He had obviously gone into a ditch and been knocked unconscious. How had he got into this bed? More important who had been responsible for removing his shirt and trousers – he was in his vest and pants!

It may be a sign of recovery that David began to fantasise over the possibility that the attractive young woman had been involved. As he turned over the bed creaked, maybe a give-away sign that he was in the land of the living, because the young woman appeared at the door.

"You are better?" she inquired.

"Yes much. But look I'm 'David'. What are you called? I ought to know."

"My name is Caterina Popescu. People call me Cati. And you are David?"

"David Edwards, I'm a representative with an English company. We do business with your Enterprises."

"And you were travelling back to Bucharest? Why do you travel so late?"

David explained about the passport.

"Yes you cannot stay without your passport. But you are all right here because we do not have to say that you were here, in fact we must not say that you are here unless we report your presence to the police. We do not wish to do that, so please when you get back to Bucharest you do not say you were with us."

"Then I must get back as quickly as possible." David made to get out of the bed but realised that all was not right when a distinct wave of dizziness came over him. Cati rushed forward.

"You must not get up yet. You must stay in bed until tomorrow morning."

"But I don't want to put you in any trouble."

"There will be no trouble, you say that you slept in your car on the way back. They would not expect you to make the journey in one night."

At that moment her mother came into the room and spoke to Cati, looking across at David with a smile a couple of times. Cati smiled back at her and then nodded.

"My mother thinks that you should relax and have a good night's sleep. She has asked that I look after you."

David felt a slight increase in his heartbeat. "And how do you intend to do that?"

Cati moved closer. "I could comfort you if you wish."

"Be my guest." David did not know what she meant but it seemed to be a step towards getting to know her better. What he wasn't expecting was what followed.

133

Without turning a hair, Cati pulled off her heavy top and skirt and wearing only a chemise, slipped under the eiderdown beside him. Her arm came around him and her face was close to his. Turning towards her, he was in a position to receive her kiss on the lips.

What followed seemed like a dream when he looked back on the experience. The encouragement would have caused a calamity if he had been in full health but slightly damaged as he was, it was prolonged so that both could enjoy the event until climaxes were reached. Then, as if this were the object of the exercise, he dropped into a deep sleep, still embraced but happy.

It was light when he awoke. Slightly confused, he tried to re-orient himself. It all then came back to him and he started to draw together the events of the previous day and night.

He became aware that he was not alone in the bed. It was a strange smell, but not an unpleasant one. It was not exactly like the smell of the Romanian country dancers from the penthouse restaurant of the Bucharest Intercontinental Hotel. No, this was a mixture, a milky feminine smell and honest to goodness soap. He turned and looked at the face lying next to him. Her almost-black hair was draped partly across the pillow and partly across her pear shaped face, a face typical, he thought, of many of the Romanians that he had recently met.

He noticed, perhaps for the first time, the rather rough cotton chemise covering a slim arm that was just visible over the blanket. She was sleeping peacefully, but began to stir. The arm that was half covered by the blankets was suddenly around him. It was an unconscious movement. Her eyes were still closed and there was a look of peacefulness in her expression. At that moment he seemed a world away from the events of his last month in Romania. As he lay there, he tried to reflect on what had happened and make some sense out of what appeared to be a dream – or maybe a nightmare.

Both awake now, it was Cati who spoke first." You slept well?"

"Very well, and you helped."

She smiled. "It was not difficult. But now I must get you some water so that you can wash and be off." She slid out of the bed and, scooping up her top and skirt, turned only for a smile before disappearing though the door. David lay there relaxed as never before. His fortune seemed to change by the minute.

The door reopened and Cati appeared carrying a jug of steaming water, a towel and some clothes, which he assumed were his, which she placed on the table and chair beside him.

"You wash and come down stairs. We will have some breakfast." And then she was gone.

Surprised at how much better he felt, David eased himself with some difficulty out of the deep down mattress, and did his best with the small amount of hot water in the bowl. Venturing through the door he discovered a wooden staircase that led into a large area at the foot of the stairs. A man of about fifty, moustached and slightly grey was seated at a large table in the centre. He wore a waistcoat over a check shirt but looked very friendly with his broad smile. He uttered some words in Romanian.

"My father says you are welcome in our house." Cati was standing by a type of Aga stove with her mother, but had turned towards him as he entered. The man beckoned David to sit down on the chair next to him. David did so and was offered a slice from the large loaf of bread that had already been cut on a board on the table. They were joined by the mother and Cati who poured some coffee into the mugs that had been laid out.

"Please eat. You still have a long way to go to Bucharest."

"My car ….?"

"My father has repaired it so that you can drive."

"Would you thank your father for me and ask him how much I owe him."

Cati spoke a few words and the man's face clouded over a little.

"My father would be insulted if you were to offer anything for our hospitality."

"But the repair…"

"It was nothing, just a little straightening out. Now please eat."

They ate in silence for a while.

"You must go quickly now." Cati was clearing away the plates. "Before the people from the village are out on the road."

David nodded, got up and stretched his hand out to the father. "Thank you for you kindness." Cati translated and the man smiled and looked a little embarrassed. He then went across to the mother and without thinking placed a kiss on her cheek. It seemed the natural thing to do. She smiled and was obviously touched by the gesture. Cati seemed pleased and led him to the front door. For the first time he was able to view the house. Strangely enough it was not all that different from the houses he had seen at the exhibition in the park in Bucharest.

"What will you do now? "David was anxious to find out a little more about her. He realised that further contact would be impossible but felt tenderness towards her for a number of reasons, not only because of their closeness of the night before.

"I must go now to the house."

"The house?"

"The children's house." It suddenly flashed across his mind – 'the village of Bros. We are about 5 km from Piatuscu.' The children's house was the orphanage.

"You work there?"

"Yes but I do not get paid. It is, how you say, voluntary. I do it after my duty at the village school. I am the teacher there."

"Why don't you get paid?"

"Because there is no money. What is given to the house by the villagers is used to feed the children."

David was about to tell her of his visit to the orphanage when he remembered the promise he had made to Dinicu Mihail.

"Perhaps I can give some money."

"No, It is not allowed for anyone to know of the house except the village people. It would be dangerous for you and us if you even said that you knew of the house. Please let us stop talking about it and you go." She looked concerned and hurried him to the side of the house.

Standing there was his 1800. The evidence that it had been in a ditch was obvious from the scraped side panels, and doors and the wing had noticeably been straightened out.

"My father says it is alright to drive." She stood by the door expectantly. He got in and put the keys in the ignition then got out again. Getting close to her, he touched her hand.

"Thank you for looking after me." The meaning was not lost on Cati who smiled and leaned forward to place a gentle kiss on his lips. She then pulled away as he got into the car again, started the engine and gingerly drove forward over the mud in front of the house. When he reached the road he looked back and waved. She was still there. He accelerated and headed for Piatuscu knowing that he would feel better when he had passed through this fateful town. He reached it after about five minutes and thankfully all was quiet. Expecting every moment to be flagged down, he watched his speed, though he would have liked to have driven faster to get well clear of the town. He let out an unconscious sigh of relief as he saw the crossed-through sign of the town of Piatuscu showing that he had left it. Now for Bucharest.

Chapter 15

The journey was quite long, David didn't dare to stop so he was quite tired when he arrived at the outskirts of Bucharest. He passed the park where he had been approached by the young man. The few words he'd spoken, "Do they know about the children?" now meant something. But what could he do and, more importantly, should he do anything while he was still in Romania. That last thought worried him. It brought home to him how vested interests can change a person's outlook and even their moral outlook. Perhaps he should do something.

For a moment he thought of his father, strangely he often came into his mind when he had a problem to wrestle. Although he was a strict follower of the moral standpoint, as a result of his father's influence, he immediately dismissed the idea of trying to do anything in Romania. If there were anything he could do, he would do it, but not at the expense of getting picked up by the Romanian officials who had rough handled him before.

The main boulevard came into sight and he drove on to the hotel. He passed the main entrance, going on to the entrance to the underground car park. The 1800 had, as promised, been drivable, although it was a bit lopsided at the front end. Taking his bag out of the car, he climbed the stone stairs to the foyer and approached the reception for his key.

"Ah, Mr Edwards, there is a message for you." The receptionist reached to the pigeonhole and passed him a note. It was from George Fox. 'You left your coat here last visit. Can you come and pick it up before we have to pass it to the lost property, i.e. As soon as you can.'

Coat? What coat? He'd not left any coat at the Embassy Club. 'As soon as you can', that sounded ominous. As David turned to make his way to the front entrance, he noticed a familiar figure coming into the hotel. It was 'leather jacket', the 'tail' who had coshed him in the park.

The combination of the message from the Embassy and the appearance of the familiar 'tail' sent a warning light through David's head. Had 'leather jacket' seen him? From the steady walk to the reception it would appear not. Turning round quickly, David then hurriedly made his way to the main entrance of the underground car park. Once there he hurried down the stairs but, as fortune would have it, did not immediately make his way to the 1800.

What he saw caused him to stop in his tracks. Standing by the 1800 were two more men, not wearing leather jackets but their clothes had a definite uniform look about them. Turning quietly to the ramp exit, he crept up the concealed side alley and out into the street. He reached the Embassy with some relief and tried the Club door. The Club was not open at that time of day, it was just after 5 o'clock, and so he went up to the front entrance.

The receptionist recognised him from the evenings that he had spent in the Club, but David couldn't remember her name.

"Ah, David. Mr Fox is expecting you." She lifted the telephone and announced him. Within a few seconds George Fox appeared. His smile seemed a little strained.

"Thanks for coming so quickly. Come through." With this he turned quickly and made his way back up the high ceilinged corridor, past the balustrade staircase to his office. David followed and, once inside, was beckoned to sit down. He had never been in this part of the Embassy before and was impressed with the grandness of the large rooms with their French windows and high ceilings.

"You didn't stop at the Comercial Hotel in Resita then?" George looked worried. David explained the sequence of events and noticed that the expression on George's face remained unchanged. He left out the personal events, feeling that this would only complicate things even more.

"And you stopped on the way to Resita, outside Piatuscu." By way of explanation he went on, "A farm worker saw your car parked in a turn off from the main road and reported it to the police." As further explanation he added, "Everyone tries to ingratiate themselves with the police in case they find themselves in trouble at some time." David explained that he had stopped as a result of the call of nature and then, sensing that he ought not hide anything, mentioned the visit to the orphanage.

George went quiet and David thought it better not to interrupt his chain of thoughts. After what appeared to be lifetime, George again addressed him, still with his serious expression.

"David, luckily I believe that the fact that you actually went into the orphanage has not yet come out, but that is not to say it won't. The fact that you were also involved with someone who works in the orphanage wouldn't help."

It was David's turn to talk now. "But George, the conditions in that orphanage were terrible. Young children just lying there not making a sound and in filthy conditions too. Surely something should be done about it?"

"We know, we know, David." George looked a little embarrassed. "The children could not move because they are tied to their cots. They have all but been abandoned by the State. If it weren't for the people that you met they would just perish. We know about it but it is not a politically acceptable subject to raise at this moment."

"When will it be a politically accepted subject?" David felt himself getting a little angry.

"David," George was looking sterner now, "In politics you only take on confrontations that you can win. Merely raising issues has no place in the diplomatic service unless you can achieve something. And in this case there is nothing that can be achieved, Ceauşescu has too firm a hold. We've known about the orphanages for years. Many of the children there are the offspring of gypsies that Ceauşescu has got rid of. Others are mentally disabled children. We know the conditions are bad but there is nothing we can do." He looked embarrassed now.

David was at a loss for words. The thought that this could continue was horrifying.

"But there is something more important to sort out." George had recovered his composure. "While you were away from Bucharest, the pressure to find someone to stand trial in the Golescu case has increased. Harry's disappearance has not helped and whilst I don't think that he was involved, the success that he had with some of the construction contracts gives the authorities some food for thought. In his absence it is pretty certain that they will target you for possible arrest and trial. If it came out that you had had any involvement with orphanage personnel that would be the final nail in the coffin. And I don't just mean that as a figure of speech."

David's head was whirling. What had he done to get into this position? Again the North Circular Road started to look an attractive place to be at that moment. He felt that he had to mention that he had seen 'leather jacket' at the hotel and told George how he'd given him the slip.

George nodded. "That only confirms my opinion that you should leave Romania until all this blows over. Obviously we have to be kept out of anything that looks as if we are interfering with the course of justice but that doesn't mean that we will leave you high and dry. In the first instance I am proposing that some of your things are collected from your room, in particular your passport. In a minute I would like you to make a list of the essential items you need. Next we must look at the best way for you to leave the country."

David didn't know what to say and just nodded, waiting to hear the next step of the planned action.

"Siggie has been made aware of the situation and I have asked him to come here after his appointments. I expect him to be here within half an hour."

"How does Siggie fit into this?" David recalled the sausage skin buyer mentioning that he covered the whole of Eastern Europe and Outer Mongolia.

"Siggie can curtail his visit here and return to Hungary. That won't cause any ruffles, he does this all the time. He has his BMW here and, rather than you trying to exit by Otopeni Airport, it is suggested that you travel with him. He also has some suggestions about passports, but we do not wish to know about those. Now, while we are waiting for Siggie why don't we have some tea?" George smiled. He was back on his usual form. Afternoon tea, the diplomats' panacea for all ills. He rung a bell and requested tea and biscuits from the same lady that David had met at the reception. It duly arrived. David set about writing a short list of the essentials he would need from the hotel room, as George had suggested. There wasn't much other than his passport as he still had the overnight bag that he had taken with him to Resita.

During the time that followed George engaged David in some small talk. David told him about the Romanian family that had helped him. Although the memory of the pleasures in the deep feather mattress with Cati was still fresh in his mind, David didn't think that it was prudent to talk about them. If only things were different. Dismissing these thoughts, David gave details of his stay at Cati's family's farmhouse and the way in which the father had repaired the damaged car. It was at this point that the phone bell rang and Siggie was announced.

Siggie bounced in, hand outstretched to George and then to David. "How are you guys?" He had obviously learnt all his English from an American contact, most likely a girlfriend, David thought.

"Fine, Siggie," George responded. "Now your trip tomorrow. You are off to Hungary through the Dradea border crossing?" Siggie nodded.

"You know the situation with regard to David?" Siggie nodded again. "Well, it is even more complicated. David inadvertently got spotted parked in the vicinity of one of the orphanages. What isn't known yet, is that he's been inside of one."

Siggie whistled. "That could cause some problems."

"So you can see that it would be prudent for David to make a hasty exit."

Siggie intervened quickly. "He's welcome to come with me. Better than trying to get out through Otopeni."

"I wonder if they will pick him up at the border crossing."

"I think that we can cover that," Siggie looked at George knowingly.

"But you don't want to know anything about that do you?"

"Best not to." said George. "So I suggest that David stays here tonight and you pick him up early tomorrow. All right?"

"Fine by me, but we need to have some time together tonight. Is there somewhere quiet where we can get in a huddle privately?"

"You can have the interview room. Anything you need?"

"You wouldn't have some gum, I mean paste for sticking paper and some scissors would you?"

"That can be arranged." George opened the door and led David and Siggie along to the interview room. The room was similar to George's office with a high ceiling, French windows, furnished with plastic topped tables and wooden armed chairs. No sooner had they settled down than George re-appeared with the paste and scissors.

"Give a shout if there is anything else you want." Then he disappeared.

"David. I think that it will be difficult for you to get through the border as David Edwards. I think that there is a fair chance that because it is unusual for Brits to go by road to Budapest, they may hold you while they check on you." Siggie was unusually serious. David was beginning to feel even more uncomfortable.

"But I go through so regularly that I don't cause a stir. And if I have a German colleague with me that will also not be so unusual, it has happened before. Now, because I do not wish to always disclose whom I have visited and where I have been, I hold two passports. I believe that if one of those passports carries your photo it can be used as a German colleague's passport."

"The only photo I have is on my passport. No wait a minute." David thrust his hand into his inside pocket and pulled out his wallet. He had remembered that he had had to have a photo attached to the student pass when he was attending the evening language course at the Polytechnic. He fished this out and sure enough it was a passport size photograph.

"Great." exclaimed Siggie pulling the passport out of his bag and sizing it over the photograph area. "Muller is not an uncommon name in German. And as long as the picture matches your dial, they won't query anything." He proceeded to cut out David's photograph and, easing off his own photograph, he glued the new photograph in place.

"You speak a little German?"

"A little."

"O.K. Put a few words together."

David thought then blurted out one the standard phrases he had learned.

"Ich bin sehr dankbar für Ihrer Helfe."(I am very grateful for your help.)

"Great. That sounds O.K., so use it when I say something to you at the border or if we are stopped. So, we should be O.K. to leave about at 7.30 a.m. tomorrow. You are stopping here tonight?"

"I think so." It was all moving a bit fast for David.

"Good. Look I'm buzzing off now. Got to get things wound up and I have a chick to meet at the Corinthian, which might see me late in bed tonight – or earlier if I have my way." Siggie was back in his exuberant mode. "See you at 7.30 a.m. then." He shook David's hand and turned to go out. At the door he turned again. "Don't worry kid. Have a good night's sleep. Pity you don't have a chick too; it would take your mind off things."

It wasn't until after he had gone that it struck David that Carol might be back. In a way he hoped that she wasn't. Stress can make a difference to the level of a man's libido. He had never yet failed to rise to the occasion – even twice on a couple of occasions, but he didn't want to fail now.

George re-appeared. "Everything settled. No don't tell me about it. Come I will show you to your room. We eat at 7 o'clock so you have time to shower or what."

David needed to know. "Is Carol on duty at the moment?"

"No, sorry old man. She went down with 'flu back in Blighty. Not returning until next week. Hard luck. You got on with her well didn't you?" That's putting it nicely thought David, very definitely relieved.

David followed George up the staircase, which was familiar from his last visit with Carol, to a room on the other side of hers. It was furnished in a similar fashion, divided into two with the bed and the shower cubicle the other side of the partition.

"Have a little rest and brush up. I will give you a knock at about 7 o'clock." David looked at his watch – 5.45. He had time to take half an hour's rest and then shower. When he awoke he found that he had dozed for longer than he had intended. It was 6:50. Hurriedly he had a tepid shower and got dressed, changing into the overnight shirt he had taken, but not worn, on his visit to Resita.

Promptly, on the stroke of seven, there was a knock on the door. David opened it to greet George, complete with jacket and tie.

"Ready old chap? Let's be off to the dining room." David followed him down the stairs and past the offices to the back of building where there was a larger room set out with tables for six.

The meal that followed was the best meal that he had had in all the time that he had been in Romania. The inevitable pork, but this time cooked in a pasta dish with a creamy sauce. This was followed by a sort of roly poly pudding and then some cheese. The meat dish was accompanied by some white wine, which again was the best he had tasted in Romania. They obviously knew their wines, thought David. The other people who joined their table were pleasant enough company, but obviously not reared in Dagenham nor went to grammar school. Their conversation centred around sport: cricket and rugby. David introduced soccer into the conversation; although there was polite interest his companions were as much out of their depth as David was in talking rugby. All that he knew about rugby was that the main aim of international rugby matches was to beat Wales.

After the meal was over they all crossed over to the Club. It was beginning to get visitors from the West and soon George was pre-occupied in acting the genial host to all, especially the new chap who had just arrived from Sweden. After a few drinks, David decided that he ought to get an early night and George gave him instructions on where to get breakfast in the morning and promised a wake-up call for 6.15 a.m. After such an eventful day, it was not surprising that David was soon asleep.

Chapter 16

David woke up just before 6 o'clock, so he was wide awake when George knocked. He acknowledged the knock and quickly got dressed, washing in the hand basin. Downstairs he was surprised to find so many of the embassy staff already serving themselves with scrambled egg and bacon from the heavy sideboard in the dining room. Then he remembered that everyone started work early in Romania and finished early to compensate.

"All ready for the trip?" George asked almost nonchalantly. David nodded having just taken a mouthful of scrambled egg.

"When you get to Budapest ask Siggie to drop you at the embassy and they will sort you out an air ticket for the flight home. Now, must dash." He extended a hand, which David grasped, and he watched him disappear through the big doorway just as Siggie arrived.

"All set?" Siggie was standing with his car keys in his hand.

"You are not taking breakfast?"

"No I am not into the English cooked breakfast. A cup of coffee does me until about 11 o'clock. That's when I'm about recovered from the night before." He gave a knowing wink.

David returned his empty plate to the sideboard. "I'll just go and get my bag". He collected the hand luggage that he had packed the night before and returned to find Siggie outside in the forecourt of the club building, standing by his BMW.

"Right, off we go." David put the bag in the boot, which Siggie had opened, and climbed into the passenger seat. He was immediately impressed with the luxury in the car – leather upholstery and wood fascias. Siggie slid in and, without much of a sound, started the three-litre engine and glided out of the embassy iron gates, turning right up the Boulevard Mageheru and heading out of the city. Once on the move, Siggie relaxed a bit.

"Your first experience of Romania has not been a very happy one."

"You can say that again. How do you put up with all the hassle?"

"Well, it's different for me." Siggie smiled. "They need me so I don't have to haggle so much in the negotiations. I tell them what I will pay for the sausage skins and then the only discussions are about how they will get paid."

"How they will get paid?"

"Yes "continued Siggie, "with currency rates changing all around the markets I am involved with, I can often make twice as much profit by paying in a different currency, depending on their rates. Also knowing what currencies the Romanian want gives me the opportunity to make an extra Deutschmark or two."

David was impressed. Siggie was obviously a very astute businessman in spite of his philandering.

"And," Siggie continued, "the Romanians are basically very nice people, very loving – and I don't just mean the women, although that is true there as well. It is the oppression of the Communist regime that causes them to act in the way that they do."

David didn't find this hard to believe after his experience in Bros.

"But what about the children's homes? Do you know about these?"

"Yeah, although they keep very quiet about them. Frightened to say too much, you know. But from what I have heard there are people trying to look after them as best they can and for 'gar nicht'." This was a German expression that David knew: it meant completely nothing. His mind turned back to Cati.

"Siggie." A thought has struck him "We have to go through Bros, Would you mind if we stopped for a few minutes?"

"Is that where you stopped overnight?"

"Yes."

"Do you think that is wise? I mean you could be putting the family at risk."

"Could we find some excuse for calling in on them?"

Siggie thought for a moment then came up with an idea. "If you can tell me when we are a little way from the house, I will pull up and open the bonnet. Then you can go to the house ask for some water for the radiator. Be sure to come back with a jug or something."

Relieved David nodded. They motored on, initially both in deep thought, then the conversation turned to Siggie's exploits and David was treated to a host of stories on 'the chicks' that Siggie had conquered. David realised that he was not in the same league, but having heard that his dalliances had given Siggie syphilis twice, though he had been cured with a course of injections after some suffering, David was pleased that he had kept to his little circle of acquaintances.

It made him think of Sheila and he wondered what the situation would be when he arrived back in the UK. Strangely he felt a little more warmly towards her than he had been before he left for Romania. Looking back at the road, David began to recognise some of the passing landmarks. There was the pull over and the lane where he had relieved himself. Cati's house could only partly be seen though the trees. About a half a mile further on he asked Siggie to pull over. Siggie got out and opened the bonnet; he nodded to David who swiftly got out of the car and began walking towards the isolated house where he had stayed.

Once there, he knocked on the door, once again recalling that the house was not very different from the ones that he had seen in the exhibition in the park. His memory went back to his strange experience in the park but now he could relate to the cries of the young man.

To his delight, and somewhat to his surprise, the door was opened by Cati. Her face fell and he could see fear in her eyes.

"Don't worry Cati, I have a good excuse to be here if anyone asks." He explained the ruse of getting water for the radiator of the BMW. "Please could you get me a jug or pot and fill it with water. I'll wait here." She went inside and some minutes later returned with an earthenware jug. David took it.

"I need to talk to you quickly." David took the jug. "I am going back to England but I want to help with the children."

"There is nothing you can do, nothing anyone can do." Cati was almost crying.

"I think that there is. Some time in the future we may be able to come to Romania and make improvements; in the meantime we can make people aware of the situation and the Red Cross or other organisations may be able to get some things into Romania. I need to know how many children there are and where they are. Do you know that?"

"I know most of them." Her face had brightened.

"While I go back to the car can you make out a list of the ones that you know? I'll be back in a short while with the jug."

"I will do that."

David took the jug and returned to the car. Siggie was putting on a presentable act that would convince any passer buy that he had a radiator problem. He poured some water in and closed the bonnet. Starting the car again, they drove to the house and knocked at the door. Cati appeared and, without a word, surreptitiously passed David a scrap of paper. She took the jug and closed the door.

It was a pity that the relationship could not continue, thought David, but he was now resigned to the problems of Romania and how different it was from the Western Europe.

"David, Are you sure you know what you are doing?" Siggie asked, as he watched David looking through the list.

"Certainly." David felt a little glow inside. At least he wasn't sitting back helpless like everyone else he had met who knew about the awful situation of the children. He may not achieve anything, but at least he would try to help. They motored on. Siggie was a good driver but kept his foot hard on the accelerator, racing through the villages at 70 miles an hour; it was hair-raising.

As they were passing through one village a policeman stepped off the edge of the pavement and furiously waved his truncheon at Siggie. Siggie replied by waving back. "See I told you that they were friendly people." David looked back through the wing mirror and saw that the policeman had stopped waving and was getting into his green Police Dacia.

"Siggie, that policeman who was waving…"

"Yes, friendly lot of guys aren't they?"

"No Siggie, he's got into his police car."

Siggie gave a laugh "They can have their little ride but a Dacha chasing a BMW?" His foot went a little harder on the accelerator and the BMW leapt forward. David had to smile; he had never met such an extrovert. But the smile left him when two miles out of the village they came up against a line of farm vehicles all queuing at a railway crossing barrier, obviously waiting for an oncoming train. There was no way that Siggie could get passed them. All that he could do was to drive up alongside the tractor at the front so that he could speed off as soon as the barrier lifted. In the rear view mirror David could see the green Dacia approaching. He recognised it as it drew closer as the police car that they had sped past a little way back.

Chapter 17

"Christ Siggie. They've caught up with us."

"Say nothing but if they draw out their pistols put up your hands."

How could Siggie stay so calm? They were certainly going to be in trouble. Sure enough the Dacia drew up behind them and two green uniformed policemen got out. One immediately pulled out his pistol.

"Get out slowly David and don't forget, up with the hands and closed with the mouth." Siggie was already half way out of the open car door.

"Grüss Gott." Siggie was smiling with his hands held high. The pistol-holding officer wasn't smiling. "Papieren."

David could understand what he meant, but before he had started to get out his passport Siggie whispered, "Slowly David, very slowly." David did what he was told and passed over his passport to the unsmiling man. Siggie smiled at the officers and, bending his head slightly towards the police driver said, "Fahren sie?" At the same time he rotated his hands and arms, still held up high, as if he were turning a steering wheel.

The official squinted up at him. David saw that Siggie was holding the car keys in one hand and he gently moved them towards the driver. Again "Fahren sie"? The police driver turned towards his companion and a small exchange took place. Then, to David's surprise, he put his pistol back into his holster and beckoned to Siggie to hand him the keys. Siggie's smile broadened even more.

Acting as if the policeman was a lost friend, Siggie beckoned him into the driver's seat, gave him a few instructions about the controls, and stepped back closing the driver's door. The second policeman now had his pistol out. But, with a roar, a leap forward, and a crunch of gears that made Siggie wince, the BMW took off under the now raised crossing gate and was soon disappearing up the road, leaving the farm traffic in its wake.

The remaining policeman beckoned them to sit on the grass verge. After sitting there in silence for about 15 minutes, thankfully, they could see the BMW appearing in the distance, accompanied by the roar of the revving engine. With a screech of brakes the BMW spun round by the side of the Dacha. The police driver swaggered out of the driver's door, smirking to his colleague as he came over to Siggie.

"Gut?" Siggie asked. The policeman nodded, "Schnell?" David knew that one – 'fast'. Again the nod. Reluctantly, the policeman handed Siggie back the car keys. Then, most surprisingly, the aspiring Grand Prix driver raised his hand in a salute and turned back towards the police car.

"Does than mean we can go?"

"Just wait until they drive off and don't forget to smile and wave." Siggie was already poised for the wave. The policeman gave a further salute, turned his car round, and started back the way they had come.

A little further on they stopped to fill the large capacity tank of the 3 litre car. David still had butterflies in his stomach. The pump attendant was a uniformed girl, slightly plump but not unattractive. Whilst she was handling the pump nozzle Siggie bent over and whispered something in German in her ear, and then stroked her arm. David could see that the girl was smiling.

"You see she loves it. I told you that they were loving people," he called to David and as she cut off the pump he placed a kiss on her cheek before going off to pay the account. What a character, David thought. With a wave to the girl, who returned the gesture, Siggie set off again, getting up to 70 mile per hour within a few minutes. It seemed as if he wasn't able to drive any slower.

Three hours later they arrived at the border, having driven through the impressive Carpathian Mountains. The border crossing was imposing, with its half-barriers straddling each carriageway of the road, forcing the traffic to move through an S bend to navigate it. On the side of the road was a concrete-lined ditch some 15 ft deep. There was no way that any vehicle could pass through the arrangement at any speed. A drab single storey square building stood to the right of the barrier ahead. Some 200 yards further on was the Hungarian frontier post, which was similarly guarded.

Two uniformed Romanian guards, one with a machine gun on a strap over his left shoulder, ordered Siggie to stop. The other guard was a woman, although it was very difficult to tell, as her uniform masked any feminine curves. Her scowl was similar to the expressions with which the customs officers had greeted David when he had arrived at Otopeni Airport. The man with the machine guard twitched his carbine, signalling that they should get out of the car.

"Get out slowly," Siggie said to David whilst he himself sidled out, "and stand by the car. Look at the guy with the gun and smile."

"Pass," demanded the woman.

Siggie turned to David and nodded. They took out their passports and passed them over to the woman who studied them, looking the two men up and down, first David and then Siggie

As she was studying the passports, Siggie leant into the car and pulled out a magazine. Turning towards the woman he opened it and turned the pages towards her. Her eyes immediately turned away from the passports and locked on the coloured pages. Siggie spoke again and moved round to lay the magazine out on the bonnet of the car. The woman went over and peered down at the pages that the smiling Siggie turned over slowly for her.

Her facial expression had changed. There was a slight smile and her eyes were glinting. Siggie continued to talk quietly then laughed a little. The woman was not smiling but was looking very intently at the pages as Siggie turned them. What the hell is he doing? David was completely confused. Then Siggie with a sweeping gesture with his hands pushed the magazine towards the woman who, with hardly a pause, picked it up and curled it into a roll.

She certainly looked more friendly now. Passing the passports back, she walked to the back of the car with Siggie and cursorily examined the boot. With a flick of her hand she beckoned Siggie to close it and walked back to the other guard. After a short word with him, she beckoned them to go through under the barrier that was now being raised.

"Let's go," said Siggie indicating to David to get back in the car. The engine started up and Siggie slowly rounded the S bend in the road past the concrete ditch and into the no man's land between the two border posts. 150 yards later the process was repeated. There was no time for David to find out what Siggie had done to get round the Romanian woman guard.

Two guards, dressed in green uniforms this time, but both with carbines motioned to them to get out of the car. Following the example of Siggie, David slid out of the BMW for the second time.

"Servus, meine Freunde," shouted Siggie. waving his hand. "Ist die Bar noch geöffnet?" One of the guards, looking a little taken back, nodded.

"Wir kommen jetz ins schöne Ungarnland. Das muß man feiern werden. Möchtet ihr alles etwas mit uns zur Begrüßung trinken?" With this he started to walk towards the building to the left of the post.

What is he doing, thought David. To his surprise the two guards had shouldered their machine guns and were walking towards him as he neared the door to the single storey building.

David hadn't understood all that Siggie had said, but he obviously had in mind inviting them for a drink. He followed Siggie, keeping a little way behind. They met other uniformed guards at the doorway. Continuing to follow Siggie, David found himself in a little bar, rather sparse but with a few chairs, a counter, and some bottles on the shelf behind it..

"Alles trinken!" bellowed Ziggie, and four of the uniformed guards gathered round the bar whilst one set out six glasses and set about pouring from a bottle of plum-coloured liquid.

"It is good Hungarian brandy," declared Siggie, responding to the cries of eggershergeray (egézségére), which David later learned passed for 'cheers' in Hungarian, by raising his glass and clinking it against that of the nearest guard. David followed suit, clinking glasses with his companions.

"Noch einmal," called Siggie, and again the bottle was brought down from the shelf and the glasses refilled. Siggie was laughing and exchanging a few words in German with two of the guards

Pulling out his wallet, Siggie placed some Deutschmarks on the counter. Then he pushed both their passports towards the one of the guards who was at the barrier.

"Alles in Ordnung?" David knew that one. 'OK?'

The guard opened both passports, made as if to examine them, and then with a friendly smile and wave handed them back. Still waving Siggie turned and, beckoning David to follow him, made his way out of the doorway pausing only to call back "Schluss"- goodbye- and returned to the BMW. By the time they were both inside the car the guard had returned to the barrier and was raising it for Siggie to negotiate. Once clear, Siggie put his foot down on the accelerator and they were soon racing free along straight and empty roads.

"Now," asked David, "tell me what all that was about."

"Oh you mean the Romanian woman. Well it was obvious, as with a lot of Romanian women in those positions, she was a Lesbierin."

"Lesbian," David corrected. "Yes a lesbian, and what I showed her was a copy of *Playboy* and a couple of pages of Playboy girls with big tits." Siggie was incorrigible, David thought. "The Romanians are not allowed to have that sort of magazine, and with a few words in her ear about her fantasies, we made a friend. Anyway, they are not worried, except perhaps in your case, about people leaving Romania, there is nothing of any value anyone can take out except currency."

David could only smile. "How did you know that the Hungarians would be so friendly?"

"Ach! Because they don't like the Romanians and remember they tried to break away from communism in 1956. Since that time they have never been quite so committed. Besides they like a drink "

"They understood your German?"

"You forget, David, that their heritage goes back to the Austro-Hungarian Empire. German was the second language before the Russian influence and many of the older Hungarians still speak it."

They were making good time and the villages and towns flew by. David was feeling a little drowsy and at one point he lost a few miles dozing. They came to the outskirts of Budapest quicker than he had expected.

"George Fox thought that it would be better if you were taken to the British Embassy. I have been there but they don't have an Embassy Club." Noticing David's surprise, he continued, "It is not quite so bad here as in Bucharest, although one still has to be careful."

Crossing the Danube, the BMW finally came to rest at a large imposing building. Siggie stopped at the gated entrance guarded by green uniformed men and an English person in a navy double-breasted jacket. Having been announced, the BMW was allowed to drive into the semi-circular drive to the house.

As Siggie and David got out, the large door opened and a tall well-groomed man appeared. He came over and held out his hand to David.

"Hello David, Cedric Houseman, Second Secretary. Welcome to Budapest." The voice was stereotype English and the smile was genuine. Cedric turned towards Siggie, "Herr Muller, Thank you very much for your help with David's problem." Siggie looked embarrassed. "I think that it was better that he was out of Romania in view of the difficulties."

"Yes and you were a great help. Thanks awfully." David winced at the expression but Cedric appeared to be genuinely grateful.

"Time to say goodbye, David." Siggie looked solemn, an unusual expression for him. David felt a lump in his throat and, grasping Siggie's hand he put his other warmly round his shoulder, and Siggie reciprocated.

"Siggie, Thanks for everything. We'll be in touch"

"We sure will, and when you start something on those children homes, let me in on the act." The smile and cavalier attitude was back. David wondered what 'chick' he had lined up in Budapest for that night.

David waited until the BMW was out of the gates and out of sight before following Cedric into the embassy. From the furnishings, it could have been the embassy in Bucharest.

"Now David, I expect that you would like to have something to eat. But first let me show you to your room. We felt that it would be better for you to overnight here before your flight tomorrow."

"Flight tomorrow?"

"Yes. We've managed to get you booked as a diplomatic courier on the Malev flight to Heathrow. Is that OK."

Is that OK? David felt as if a weight had been lifted from his shoulders. He followed Cedric in a daze up a staircase to a room that seemed somewhat familiar. Then he recognised the layout and the furniture; it was the same as in Carol's room. It seemed light years ago that he had been there.

For the meal that followed he had the company of six embassy staff; it was very pleasant and the small talk was of the UK and the latest in sport. Rugby took precedent over soccer! They're a pleasant enough crowd, David thought. He was not used to the accent, but he supposed that in the circle that they moved in, everybody talks like that.

On the journey back to Heathrow he pondered on what he was going to do after he had told K.M. that they could keep their reps job in Eastern Europe. The only good thing that had come of it was David's new-found knowledge of the orphanages, knowledge that he would not let go un-broadcast.

PART II

Chapter 1

David was in the kitchen. He was laying out the breakfast things, as he usually did. He was half-listening to the radio. It was his usual routine. He got up about 6.30 a.m., made the tea and laid out the breakfast things whilst his nearest and dearest stirred some life into their children – Christopher aged 8 and Sophie, 6.

It was still dark, but it would get lighter now that they had just passed the shortest day of the year – December 21st 1989. "...and now for a news flash, received from Reuter just over an hour ago." David's attention turned to the radio.

"It has just been reported that President Ceauşescu, the Romanian Republic President, and his wife have been caught by members of the uprising attempting to flee their residence in Bucharest and have been executed. This follows the uprising that began in Timişoara in West Romania last week when demonstrators prevented the arrest of the popular Protestant minister for defending the rights of the ethnic Hungarians."

"Sheila, Sheila," David called excitedly up the stairs, "it's happened."

"What's happened?" Sheila's voice was full of apprehension and she came hurrying down.

"Ceauşescu is dead. It has finally happened."

"When did you hear that?"

"It was just on the news." They both waited to hear the follow on. Apparently the army had done nothing to prevent the crowd from taking Ceauşescu away and the latest report was that he had been executed by members of the uprising. Noises from upstairs demanded Sheila's attention, but her face was as flushed with excitement as David's.

"You know what this means?" Sheila nodded her head in acknowledgement.

"We can now get in to do something positive."

"Oh David, do you really think so?"

David was desperately trying to pull all his thoughts together and imagine what was now possible .

Since his return from Romania some 14 years before, he had campaigned for support for his Romanian Orphan Fund. It had been difficult at first. Politics came into play, with people trying to hush up the stories that David had managed to piece together from various clandestine reports. From these reports he had estimated that about 150,000 children were being kept in old hospitals and orphanages throughout Romania. Like Hitler, Ceauşescu had wanted to get rid of the gypsies, and many of the orphans were of Romany origin. Aids was also a serious threat in the orphanages.

Over the years David had gradually built up a huge number of contacts, in America, Holland Germany. In Sweden fund raising had been taken place ready for the day when some practical help could be given. There were contacts even in Romania, but these were known only to himself. Siggie the sausage skin man had helped there as well, as with making contacts in Germany.

"I wonder if we can meet up with Dimitru." David was already planning a sortie into Romania. Sheila had had to go back to her duties with the children, but the excitement was still evident on her face when she came down with the terrible two for breakfast.

"What's happened Daddy?" Sophie was slightly confused, making her not a little worried. She'd never seen her parents so worked up.

"Well darling, it is a little difficult to explain but I'll try." Christopher was now all ears, standing beside his mother, mouth open. "Romania is a country like England but bigger. There was a bad man there who made people do what he wanted. He was also nasty to children and locked them away in big houses with not a lot of food. Now he is dead and the people can do something about the children, but they need help, money and other things. Mummy and I have been working with other people to get some money and things which we can now take to them."

"Why couldn't you take them before?" The inevitable 'why' question. Whatever you told them, there would be that inevitable 'why'.

"Well we just couldn't," and, as if to stall any supplementary 'why' questions, David went on, "come and sit down and eat your breakfast otherwise we will be having corn flakes for lunch."

"You can't have corn flakes for lunch, silly," Sophie was always the logical one.

They sat down and soon the chatter veered towards Christmas presents and Santa Clause and who was coming for Christmas. As soon as breakfast was over, David helped Sheila clear away whilst the children watched the children's programmes on the television. The Christmas programmes had already started with the traditional repeats of Walt Disney favourites such as Snow White.

David's mind flew back over the 14 years that had sped past since his visit to Romania. He had got back together with Sheila for purely physical reasons. What had surprised him was the concern about him that Sheila had shown and the depth of her interest in his story about the orphans. He had begun to see her in a new light. He had always accepted her as an intelligent person – she couldn't hold down her job as a social worker without being bright. Although she never discussed her work with him in detail, he knew that she had to handle some difficult and demanding cases.

It was partly her encouragement that had led him to set up an association of influential people to make plans for some action for the orphans. As time went by David had become more keen to spend time with Sheila – the night out with the boys was getting a little boring, perhaps because the eligible circle of girls was shrinking! In the end it seemed a good idea to enter into the state of marriage and Sheila seemed to be a good choice for a partner. As a result, some two years after David got back from Romania, he finally popped the question and received the answer that he'd expected.

"I always knew you'd end up with Sheila," his know-all mother had commented when David told her of the acceptance. His marriage had been a success, much more than he had imagined, and the depth of his feeling had increased with the arrival of Sophie and then Christopher. Sheila's encouragement in all he tackled was something he enjoyed and she was always ready to support him with the endless correspondence and telephone calls for his orphan campaign.

"I am sure that Krone will give me some time off to go over."

"I am sure they will, David."

After returning from Romania, David had joined Krone Chemicals as their Western Counties technical representative; their offices were convenient for the new marital home – Slough, in Buckinghamshire. Within four years he had progressed to Special Accounts Executive and he now had a good reputation with Krone Chemicals and their Swedish parent company.

"I wonder how Dimitru is." Dimitru was David's main contact in Bucharest; he had been feeding back information through Siggie for the past ten years. As his thoughts about what could now be achieved were swirling about his head, the telephone rang.

"Hi David." It was the strongly accented voice of Lucy, the American contact for the fund. "How about the news? Isn't it great?" Lucy was in her 50's and contacted David after having heard of the orphan fund from his German contacts; since then she had been rallying support in the States.

"Now's the time for action. Can you set up a meeting next week at a place somewhere near you? I'll take on the contact job and telephone Heinz, Jean Paul, and Josh. You can make contact with your BBC people. Next week we should set the wheels in motion to get some supplies together and make our first visit. Oh, and see if you can get Siggie to contact Dimitru to find out where we should visit first."

"David," her voice was breathless with excitement, "we can now really do something for those children." In the last few words he could hear the emotion creeping into her voice.

"OK Lucy. I'll set things up and fax you." The emotion was beginning to get to him too.

"Don't waste any more money on telephoning. I'll be in touch."

Sheila returned from checking the children. "David. Why not go in and see Mr Johannson and get clearance for time off. You can catch him today before he goes back to Sweden. I am sure that he will be sympathetic. He might even want to become involved in some way."

Good old Sheila, supportive as ever. Slightly out of character, he grabbed her and threw his arms around her drawing back only after giving her a kiss.

"I may be away for a couple of weeks," he looked for approval.

"I know, but David, this is only the beginning. Think of what can be achieved."

He hugged her again. "Now to see Johannson."

Chapter 2

"Christ. Nothing seems to have changed."

The comment was really not addressed to anyone, but John the co-driver turned to David with questioning eyes.

"Sorry John, but it seems just the same as when I passed through here some fourteen years ago. I thought that with all the other changes this would have changed as well"

They had just passed through the manned Hungarian border where they were warmly greeted and, having reached the Romanian border post, were now being addressed by the dark-blue-uniformed woman. Her attitude was far from welcoming. David recalled the previous occasion when he passed through from the other direction, when Siggie had persuaded a similar woman to go easy on them by pandering to her lesbian tendency with a copy of *Playboy*.

"You have only things for the orphanages? No alcohol, cigarettes?"

"We have only the permitted bottle of Scotch per person and no cigarettes."

"You can leave one bottle here so that we can check it. We will return it to you after we have analysed a small sample."

No, nothing had changed, thought David. Ceauşescu may be dead but the corruption lives on. Dutifully he handed over the duty free bottle of Scotch, knowing full well that that was the last time that they would see it. After further scowls and poking, the transit vans, loaded with the relief items, were beckoned through. David breathed a sigh of relief but wondered what else might hinder them from making changes to the situation he'd seen when he was here last.

The convoy of two transit vans had left London three days before. John, his co-driver of the first van, at 46 years of age, was his senior by seven years. His life as a 'chippy' had been fairly uneventful, as he had never really been very ambitious or adventurous. An annual holidays in Cornwall was the extent of the changes to his routine, perhaps the reason why his marriage had broken up some five years before.

There were no children to the marriage, something that John had always regretted. That may be why, when John saw some of the limited publicity that David had been able to give to his orphanage project, he had come forward and asked to join the party. David, recognising the value of his carpentry skills, was only too pleased to have him on board, but made it clear that there could be no reimbursement for his time. John had readily accepted the offer.

The second van was driven by Kate, a 50 year old teacher at a special needs school in South London. Her strong character was obvious as soon as one met her. Well built with a commanding air, she was every inch a person you wouldn't want to get on the wrong side of. David had taken to her immediately, feeling that there would come time when her natural authority would come in very handy.

Her co-driver, taking a year off after completing his university degree in sociology at Sheffield University, was the youngest of the group. At first Michael's offer to come had been turned down, mainly due to his age. But his persistence had won David over and he and Kate had since struck up a very good relationship.

Now through the border, the next stop was Bros, the village where Cati lived. David recalled the 'hospitality' given by Cati when he was there 12 years ago. But things had changed since then. He was happily married to Sheila, and he had heard that Cati had married a local boy in the village. Still, it was a lovely memory.

Once through the border the convoy moved steadily along the narrow main road, regularly slowing down to pass one of the many tractors. The field work was in full swing for the autumn harvesting in August. David noticed that there were still fields of sunflowers, all with the heads facing the sun. It was a memory he never forgot.

Once they had entered the village, David turned off the road, making his way down the track to the house. He wondered if anything there had changed. The door had opened before he got out of the transit, and he recognised Cati's mother. Smiling, but looking a little older, she turned back and called something out in Romanian; David assumed that she was calling for her husband. Before David was halfway up the path to the wooden house, which again struck him as very like those he had seen in Parcul Herăstrău park, Cati's father rushed down and embraced him with a kiss on both cheeks. Taken by surprise, David could only take his hand and smile.

"Caterina?" David posed the question.

Mr Popescu nodded still smiling and, taking David's hand, led him out of the gate and down the street to another house some three or four doors down. He knocked and called and finally Cati came to the door. Again there was the embrace and the kiss on both cheeks.

"Steady David,' he thought, but the kiss this time was somewhat different from their last encounter.

"I am so glad to see you David." Cati was still very attractive. "I am so pleased that you could come. Come, please meet my husband."

It was then that David noticed a man of about his own age or a little older standing in the doorway.

"How do you do." It was the familiar formal English greeting.

"This is Nikki David learned later that this was short for Nicolae, "my husband."

"How do you do." Again the formal greeting. He must have learned his English from some outdated English course. "I am pleased to meet you. And happy that you are trying to help the children."

"Cati has already done so much, so we hope that we can be of some help." Turning towards Cati he said, "I have some helpers with me. Is there somewhere we can stay for a few nights? We can pay for the accommodation."

"That will not be necessary. We have made arrangements for your companions with some people in the village, but of course you will stay with us. Please tell your friends to bring their vehicles", he remembered her using that word 'vehicle' all those years ago, "to the house on the corner of the road, there." She pointed a little further down the road to where there was a smaller road leading off it.

With that she took his hand and lead him back to the vans.

Slightly embarrassed, David introduced the crew. Even perhaps more embarrassed was Michael who was obviously taken by the black haired beauty who now stood smiling before him.

"I am pleased to meet you and welcome to Romania. We are grateful for you being here." With that she indicated to them to take the vans to the corner of the street.

When they knocked at the door of the house that she had pointed out, it was opened by a rounded full-faced woman of about 50. The welcome of the smile was again apparent and, stepping aside, she beckoned them in.

David stood aside first for Kate and then John, ushering Michael in after them. The house was similar to that of Cati's: one big room with a large table and a sink on one side. There were also two chairs and a bench type of seat on each side of a fireplace in which was an oven with an iron pot on it. Whatever was in there smelled good.

"This is your hostess, Dona. You will be comfortable here and although Dona does not speak English she will understand your needs."

"I'm sure we will get by," said Kate her positive attitude already proving an asset. With that she took hold of Dona's hand and gave it a vigorous shake. The responding smile was confirmation for David that all would be well.

"There are two bedrooms upstairs, come I will show you." Cati led the way up the wooden stairs to two rooms, one with a double bed and the other with a double and a single bed.

" I am sure that your friend will be comfortable here. Dona's son is working in Budapest and her husband is gone. I mean he has died some years ago. Now you come back to our house."

"Hold on a minute Cati please." Turning towards the crew David inquired, "Everything all right?"

"We'll be fine." Kate had taken charge. "What are the arrangements for tomorrow?"

"I'll be up for you at about 9 and we can set off for the orphanage then." Then as an afterthought he said, "I don't know what we do about eating tonight."

Cati turned and said something to Dona whose face lit up as she waved them to go downstairs. Once the party was downstairs, chairs were pulled out from the big table and plates appeared. Quite animated, she almost ordered the three of them to sit down. The big iron pot came off the stove and its contents were ladled out on to the plates. As David and Cati looked on, bread appeared and spoons were presented to the three, who had sat without a word while this was going on. Dona made the sign for them to eat.

John by this time had caught up with the quick change of events. "It smells good. What is it?"

"It is a traditional Romania stew, I think that you will like it." Cati answered.

Prompted by further sign language from Dona, John and Kate took their first spoonfuls of the steaming stew. Michael was still looking a little doubtful.

"Well, this will certainly go down well." Kate was enjoying it, smacking her lips after the first few mouthfuls. "Come on Michael. Eat up. It will do you good."

Michael, still hesitant, took a small sip and then a full spoonful and looked happier once the taste had made its mark. Dona looked on and smiled.

"So we will leave you with it."

"We will be alright with Dona, don't you worry." Kate was nodding approvingly to the smiling host. Once she and David were outside, Cati's became more serious.

"David, it will not be easy at the orphanage. Things are not much improved."

"But we sent some money and the consignment of milk powder, surely that must have helped?"

"The money," Cati shrugged her shoulders. I know nothing of that and most of the milk powder has found its way on the, how do you say it, black market."

"But we received letters thanking us for all the consignments." Again Cati shrugged her shoulders. "It takes a lot to change people. But come, we must eat." On that less gloomy note they entered Nikki and Cati's small house. Nikki was there to greet them. He put his arm around Cati's waist and greeted David, "Welcome to our house."

"And now we must eat." Cati repeated and produced a similar stew to that of Dona's and they sat at the smaller table with some wine to add to the meal. David hadn't realised that he was so hungry and didn't hesitate to accept a second helping. Some apple pudding followed. David was soon very full and, with the wine, more relaxed than he had been for the last few days.

The three of them talked a little and David learnt that Nikki was a farm mechanic, servicing and repairing anything from harvest implements to tractors. He had been employed by the local co-operative farm, but now was self-employed. It appeared to give him a good living.

Cati helped at the school and still worked at the orphanage. David was disappointed to hear that many of the Communist officials still held the same positions as before. He answered their questions about his own family and the situation in England. Cati and Nikki soaked up every word he said and would have kept him talking late into the night if it hadn't been obvious from his yawns that tiredness was getting the better of him.

Cati showed him to one of the two bedrooms upstairs, but this time she did not offer to take care of him. In spite of David's old cavalier background, he would have not have had it any other way and went to sleep with pleasant thoughts of Sheila and the children.

Chapter 3

David awoke, feeling slightly disorientated, not realising where he was. His sleep had been so deep, perhaps due to the herbs in the stew or perhaps due to the fatigue that had crept up on him the night before. His reverie was broken by a knock on the wooden door, around which Cati appeared with a steaming mug of coffee.

"You have plenty of time. It is only 8 o'clock. I will bring up some hot water for your washings." Her quaint use of English made him smile and he took the coffee gratefully. Dutifully, she returned within a few minutes with a large jug of hot water and a towel. David got up and poured the hot water into the large, heavy decorated bowl on the dressing table and, taking his travelling bag out of his pack, washed and shaved. After packing everything away again, he made his way to the room downstairs.

"Nikki has gone to the farm but he will see you again this evening."

Even though he had no philandering intentions, David couldn't help admiring Cati's figure, which was slightly fuller than on his previous visit and the healthy complexion of her typically pear shaped Romanian face.

On the table was a plate with a selection of cheeses and cut meats.

"Please take your breakfast." she beckoned him to a chair.

David didn't feel very hungry but he felt that he had to show some appreciation for her hospitality. Taking some of the rough-textured bread, he found it to be very wholesome and a perfect complement to the Romanian goats' cheese. Cati sat opposite him and waited until he had nearly finished his second cup of coffee and a plateful of food before she broached the subject of the orphanage.

"It is nice of you to come, but I do not know if you can do much. The supplies you sent have not been given to the children and many of them are now very ill."

"It's no wonder that they are ill in those conditions."

"No. It is more than that. We had visitors to the orphanage during Ceauşescu's time. They were medical men with syringes. Many of the children were treated by these men but we did not know that it was not for their health but to infect them. Many of them are now very sick and will die because we are told that there is no cure for the sickness."

"So what was all this for?" David had heard about some experimentation, but he'd never really got the full story.

"They were to used as Jimmie pigs."

"You mean guinea pigs?"

"Yes, that is the word. They wanted to see the effect of the sickness. There is nothing that we can do for them."

"You bet there is. We can make what is left of their life better than it is at the moment."

Cati smiled. "That would be nice," and with that started to clear away the table.

At just before nine o'clock they walked up to the corner and the house where Kate, John and Michael were billeted. The door was opened by Kate who seemed to have taken over.

"'Morning David, morning Katrina." Turning, she proceeded to walk back into the large room where John and Michael were sitting at the big table having just finished their breakfast of bread, cheese and cold meat breakfast. Kate had just finished washing up the breakfast things.

"How's it gone?" enquired David.

"Absolutely wonderful." John nodded in agreement with Kate. "Dona's done us proud. I tried to get the recipe for the stew; I think that I have nearly got it right."

"I can help you with that." Cati looked pleased whilst Dona looked on with a big smile.

"Well you'll be back here tonight, so you may get more Romanian recipes before you go home. Come on, there's work to do."

"How far away is the orphanage?" asked Michael, looking much more at ease than when he first arrived.

"About five miles, just outside a place called Piatescu. It stands back from the road." David remembered the pathway up to the house. They went outside and boarded the Transits, Cati riding with David and John. In less than 15 minutes they came to the track leading up to a large disheartening-looking house. They pulled up outside and made their way to the front door that, surprisingly, was not locked. The inside vestibule was familiar to David, but what he had expected was some change to the smell that had hit him last time he visited. To his dismay, it was as before.

Kate looked enquiringly at David but received no response.

Cati brushed past them both and went through a doorway at the end of the hall. She returned, closely followed by a small man of about 40 dressed in loose-fitting dark clothes, his body was bent forward slightly. The whole effect was rather sinister, but the man attempted a smile. His greeting was in Romanian. Cati translated.

"Mr Domnescu says that you are welcome but he did not expect you."

"But we told his Ministry we were coming."

Cati translated to Mr D who seemed to bend even further forward.

"Apparently they have not heard from the Ministry for some weeks."

"Well, we are here and we want to see what the situation is."

With that David strode past Cati and Mr D towards the room that he'd been in before.

As he opened the door, the stench engulfed them. Nothing had changed. The room was still full of cots, each filled with a silent motionless body.

"Oh my God!" It was Kate who reacted first to the scene.

Turning to Mr D, David said, "What has happened to the children's things that we sent out, and the cots?"

Looking sheepish, Mr Domnescu said something, which Cati translated into English, to the effect that he knew nothing of anything that had been sent. Cati added that this couldn't have been the case because on one visit she had seen the packing cases.

"David, the first thing we need to do is get these poor things cleaned up. Where's Michael?"

With that Kate stomped out to the second Transit and almost dragged out Michael. Taking control, from the back of the van they carried out a large multi-coloured roll which, when carried inside and laid out on the floor at the side of the cot area, proved to be a padded play area of plastic carpet.

Tackling the first cot, Kate lifted out the child and stripped off his clothes. What was strange was that no sound came from the boy, who turned out to be about two years old.

The unventilated room was full of the stench from the urine, although it was relatively warm.

Michael, bless him, thought David, had pulled out the mattresses and begun a pile in one corner.

Kate and Michael continued with the other cots whilst David, accompanied by John and Cati, bundled Mr Domnescu into the other room at the end of the hallway. The room was almost completely bare except for a sink, a large gas stove and a refrigerator. In the corner was, what David recognised from his childhood days at his mother's house, a large copper with a gas pipe connected to a burner underneath.

"Where are the food cupboards?" Cati translated.

Mr Domnescu led them out of the room and in through another door, which exposed a comfortable furnished room with an alcove in which there was a small bed. He pointed to a cupboard on the wall. Pulling open the door of the cupboard, they could see stacked on the shelves, some coffee and other general commodities, including a tin of Nestlé dried milk – the same brand as the consignment that had been sent to the orphanage.

"Where did this come from?" Cati again translated.

Mr Domnescu, looked shamefaced and replied that a Ministry official had left it after his last visit. David realised that he was going to get nowhere pursuing this.

"John, Lets get some shelving up in the kitchen and Cati can get help in unloading the food stuff from the vans."

"Right." John was already making his way to the van to unload the wood from the overhead rack of the first Transit. Next he reached inside and pulled out his toolbox. By the time that the helpers had finished unloading the boxes of baked beans, milk powder and packets of dried children's food, John had already sawn up some of the planks and was measuring up. Back in the children's room, almost half the children were now out of their cots, and a pile of mattresses was evident in one corner and a pile of vests and other garments beside them.

"David is there somewhere we can clean these clothes? We only have enough clothes with us for half of these poor children."

Turning to Cati David asked, "Can you get the copper going and find us some soap?"

"I know where the cleaning materials are kept. When I am here I use them to clean the floors. I think that there are some soap flikes there"

David didn't think that this was the right time to correct her English.

"Good, let's get the copper going and we can get some of these filthy clothes washed."

By this time John had already put the first shelf up on one of the walls and some of the food tins were already on it. Michael, in a spare moment had returned to the van and got out the box of coloured balls and other children's play things and was spreading these on the mat beside the bemused children who were sitting there. There were already a few damp patches.

"The next thing is to prepare something to feed the children."

"I do that," said Cati. "We normally bring up some thin stew but I can make up something with what you have brought."

"We have two more vans with food coming through in a few days' time." David remarked.

Domnescu was now making agitated signs and muttering something in Romanian. Cati translated "He says that there is a delivery of pork due today from the Ministry. I have seen these and it is usually the meat that is not good enough to eat. We put this in the copper to make a thick soup. But we also have big pots in the cupboard. When it comes we can use those."

"Good, I'll go and help Kate".

The rest of the day was frantic. Luckily the windy day helped to dry out the sheets and other washed clothing. At the end of a very long day the children, who had been washed by Kate with Michael, were back in their cots. They had been fitted with nappies and lay on clean sheets, all the volunteers having helped feed them with a cup of milk made from the powder and a portion of baked beans.

At the end of the day, the tired party returned to the vans and returned to Dona's house where they welcomed the opportunity to wash in steaming hot water. Then they all sat round the big table to partake of what Kate later described as the best and spiciest chilli-con carne she had ever tasted.

The next morning, David and Cati arrived at the corner house to find the party tucking into wholesome bread and some home made jam.

"I have been talking to Cati and realise that there is little more that we can do, other than what we are doing now. When our food supplies run out and we have to leave the situation could go back to how we found it. There are, of course, the other helpers here; Cati has told me that Maria and Ana, two ladies from the village, go up to the orphanage to give the children the food but they get a rough reception from Domnescu, who they believe is on the fiddle, taking any supplies that come in from outside."

"So what is the plan?" Kate as always looked for action.

"Whilst you are coping with the children, I propose that I go to Bucharest and try to get the system of managing the orphanage changed. Cati has volunteered to form a committee to take over the running of the orphanage with her acting as the liaison with us and any other organisations that we can put in touch with her."

"I would like to stay and help." It was Michael. "I have a full year off from university and I could help with the business side as well as do something in house."

Kate's face almost split in two with the broad smile that appeared.

"That's my lad." To Michael's embarrassment she put her arms around his shoulders and gave him a hug.

"If that's what you want I am sure that Cati will be pleased to have some help." David looked at Cati who nodded enthusiastically.

"Thanks." It was Michael's turn to break out into a big smile now.

"So, first thing tomorrow Nikki will take me to the station and I will catch the train to Bucharest."

That settled, they set off for the house while John continued with work in the kitchen, building shelves and cupboards, whilst the children were taken out of their cots and washed and changed. Michael took on the task of trying to placate two of the older children, both about 7 years of age, who were very frightened when any of the strangers went anywhere near them. At the end of the day he seemed to have succeeded in getting them to involve themselves in a simple game of rolling a large plastic ball to and fro.

It was another tiring day, but at least Mr D kept out of the way.

Chapter 4

It was a new experience for David. When he had been in Romania before he had travelled by car. Although he had travelled on a continental train when he travelled to Austria for his ill-fated skiing trip, he was not prepared for the basic fittings of the Romanian trains. Thankfully, Nikki had bought him a first class ticket, which meant that he could sit on Rexene type seats rather than the wooden slatted ones of the second class.

He had the carriage almost to himself. The only other occupant was a man who David guessed to be about 50 years old, dressed in a uniform. David didn't recognise it, but his curiosity was soon satisfied.

"Guten Morgan." The words were said with a smile. The man had obviously recognised that David was not Romanian.

"Sorry, English."

David thought that he might get into complications using his smattering of German.

"Ah. So you are visiting Romania on holiday?" The man's English was slightly clipped.

David thought before he answered.

"No, we have brought some things for an orphanage.

The man's face clouded.

"I am sorry. We should have done something but it was difficult."

He looked embarrassed.

"I was here about 14 years ago for the first time, so I do know the circumstances. But I hope that it has now changed."

"In some ways, yes. But there are still some of the old guard who are fighting the change. I have been fortunate working for the railways. We were left alone and in the railway business as it was necessary to have contact with other countries. That is why many of us learned English."

"Your English is very good."

"Thank you. It is now better than before because we hear radio broadcasts in English."

"I had some dealings with your railway people. I met a Mr Mihail at the railway works in Resita."

"Mr Mihail." The way he said it reminded him of the way in which his contact on his last visit had spoken of 'JR' – the Welsh rugby star. A sort of hushed reverence.

"Unfortunately Mr Mihail died two years ago, but he was a fine man. He was also very clever and that is why the authorities tolerated him. I met him on many occasions. He had been to England. Did you know that?"

"Yes he told me that he had been to Swindon, which is our railway town."

"He spoke out just one too many times before his death and they finally broke him."

"I'm sorry?" David looked questioningly.

"He tried to get something done about the orphanage but someone who he thought he could trust informed the State Police. He was dismissed from his post and lost his house and the salary that went with the job. He was given only a very small pension and a small flat. I think that it was the loss of his involvement in the railways that broke his heart."

"I am very sorry to hear that. He appeared to be a very nice man."

"He was. But how are you involved with the orphanage?"

David briefly explained the background.

His travelling companion looked thoughtfully out of the window. After a little pause he looked at David again.

"It will not be easy. Although we have changed – I could not talk to you as I have before – there are still those who will profit from any thing."

It was as if he had said too much because suddenly he changed the subject and asked David about England. His questions were general and he was obviously not a sports fan. David chatted about his country whilst the train trundled slowly along, crossing many road crossings. David remembered the crossing that had pulled them up when he and Siggie were leaving Romania and smiled inwardly at the thought of him. Siggie still kept in touch and was working with the German supporters of the orphanage campaign.

The train arrived at Bucharest some two hours later and David said goodbye to his travelling companion.

He had been at this railway station years before, but only to get the details of a train journey in case he wanted to travel by train instead of by car. It still looked the same but this time, when he went to the taxi rank, he was able to get in a taxi and instruct the driver without the previous formality that he had experienced.

The taxi pulled up outside the British Embassy and a familiarly sloppily dressed Romanian soldier was at the gate. He was not challenged and wondered what the soldier was doing there. Through one of the big double doors, which formed the entrance, he approached the receptionist who looked up straight away.

"Good morning Sir. Can I help you?" This was different.

"Could I see the First Secretary please? It was Mr Charles Munrow the last time I was here."

"I do not know the name, sir, but I will make enquiries. Can I have your name please?" She picked up the phone and, a few minutes later, a moustached man of about 40 appeared.

"Hello, Derek Martin." He extended his hand and gripped David's firmly. "I believe you were enquiring about Charles. I am afraid he moved on a few years ago. Even before my posting, but I know of him. Is there something I can do?"

"Well, perhaps yes." Before he could continue, Derek extended his arm towards the entrance from where he had appeared.

"Let's go through to my office. Perhaps you'd like some tea whilst we are talking." Without waiting for a reply, he nodded to the receptionist who picked up the telephone to arrange this. David followed, recognising the corridor and the office that he had been in 14 years previously.

"Sit yer'self down. Now what I can I do for you?"

"We have a party working at the orphanage at Bros."

"Yes, we were advised that you were coming. From what I have heard you're doing a grand job with the International organisation. Unfortunately it is still a little sensitive a subject for us to get involved in."

David felt his hackles rise.

"Isn't about time you stopped thinking about the politics and tried to think about the children?"

Derek looked a little taken back, but immediately his diplomatic training came into use.

"Of course I can well understand your feeling but there are broader issues at stake."

"Have you been to any of the orphanages?"

"Well, actually, no."

"Then how do you know if the 'broader issues' are more important?"

Derek obviously wanted to defuse the situation.

"Look, it doesn't mean that *our* hands are tied. Is there anything I can do to help matters?"

David realised that he was talking to the monkey and not the organ grinder. But he could at least push as hard as he could to use the Embassy to get the control changed at Bros.

"Yes there is." He then proceeded to describe the situation he'd found at Bros.

"You can help me get this Domnescu bloke replaced with a village committee."

"There is a problem." Derek went on quickly, seeing David's reaction.

"Don't get me wrong. I will be only too pleased to help, but what you have to realise is that all is not as it should be. Whereas the old system has changed, many of the officials have managed either to stay in their jobs or slide into equally rewarding ones. It is therefore difficult to get things changed. There is also the corruption."

"Corruption?"

"Yes. Whereas when Ceauşescu was in power any corruption was punishable by death, it is now easier and rampant."

David felt a twinge when he remembered how it was when he was there last.

"However," Derek continued now fully recovered from his embarrassment, "we can get a meeting arranged with the Social Services department. I will set that up tomorrow. Have you booked in at a hotel?"

"No. I didn't know whether I would need to stop over."

"I'll arrange for a room at the Corinthian Palace" He pronounced it as David had heard it before – Corinthian Palass. "We have some rooms that are held for us there. We will pick up the bill for your couple of nights. Now if you can sort out your room there, we would be very pleased if you could join us this evening for dinner and enlighten us on your movement and what you are doing. O.K.?"

David realised that he needed the Embassy if he was going to make any contact at all. Recovering his composure, he replied, "That is very kind of you, Derek. Perhaps it would be useful to fill you in on the activities of the International Orphanage Group. Can I get a taxi?"

"Soon done." The diplomatic smile was back." Shall we say 6 o'clock? We can sort a few things out before we go to dinner."

Chapter 5

The Corinthian Palace hotel was similar in style to the Theodore, although a little larger. There had been some modernisation and the room that David was given was certainly not as 1920s as that at the Theodore. After settling in and having taken a shower, he wandered downstairs and passed the doors to the restaurant where he had been with Gheorghe and his infamous parcel. It seemed light years away now. Ordering a beer in the conservatory, he began to 'man watch'. He was surprised to notice how many German guests appeared to be staying there, but then he remembered that they were well entrenched when he was here last. Finishing his beer, he left to go to the Embassy. Having noted that the Corinthian Palace was only a few steps further into the city than the Theodore, he decided to walk rather than take a taxi.

Turning left outside the hotel, he could see the square opposite, which stood in front of the large building where, he had understood, Ceauşescu had sometimes resided when in Bucharest. He noticed that people were now walking in front of the building; this had not been permitted when he was there last. Then, everyone had to make a detour around the other three sides of the square to pass through. David had just passed the corner of the street into the main boulevard when he was approached by an older woman who, although addressing him in Romanian, made her request quite clear by holding out her hand.

David was slightly nonplussed. He had not seen this before in Romania; he fumbled in his pocket for any spare coins. The receipt of these brought a flood of Romanian from the old woman, who tried to grab his hand at the same time bending her head towards it. Embarrassed, David immediately retreated and circled her to continue on his way.

"Beggars are a regular sight now," explained Derek when he related the experience to him, shortly after being received at the embassy door.

"Under the previous regime, there was no unemployment and everyone received an income, small though it may have been. Now, under the capitalist system, enterprises no longer carry the surplus of workers and the State only provides the very minimum of pensions to old folk."

"On the other hand," he went on, "there are Mafia type organisations that operate all sorts of money making operations, from protection rackets to selling off the aid, such as you are providing, to those who can pay for it."

"And I thought the other regime was bad."

"It will get better, at least that's what we all think. At least we don't have the sudden disappearance of people that went on under Ceauşescu. But let's not dwell on the general, but concentrate on the specific." Derek was referring to a large booklet. "I suggest that the person you ought to see is Mr Constantin, spelled with an 'i' on the end. He is responsible for the Social Services. I don't know him, but we do know his assistant, Emunescu. He used to work here and although we knew that he fed some information back to the Romanians, we are convinced that he selected the material that was of little importance. You would do well to see him first, he may be able to give you a few tips on how to approach Constantin."

Derek reached for the grey telephone and dialled a number; David could hear the single tone from where he was sitting. After what appeared to be a long wait, a voice must have answered as Derek started to speak, asking for Mr Emunescu. Again there was a long wait.

"Mr Emunescu? Paul, how are you, Derek Martin here." Pause. "Oh all right, but things are not as well organised as when you were here." Derek smiled.

"Paul, I have a David Edwards here, you may even know him. He was here some years ago. Oh, before your time. Nevertheless, you could help him. He can explain the details himself. Are you free this afternoon? Say 11.00? Good I'll tell him how to get to you. Nice talking to you and thanks."

He hung up.

"Emunescu is O.K., within the confines that he can be, but at least he is a friendly face and I am sure that you'll profit from seeing him first. Now tell me how far you've got and then we can throw in a few thoughts on what pressure you might be able to put on Constantin."

David gave some details of the organisation and described the people he had brought with him. He then outlined the situation he had found and the fact that the aid they had already sent appeared to have 'disappeared'. He also told him of the information that he had gleaned about the experiments that had been carried out on some of the children. He reiterated his intention of trying to get the orphanage into the hands of the Bros volunteers, knowing that the children would be far better looked after if they had control of it. It would also give him confidence in the safe receipt of future aid supplies.

Derek listened without making any comment.

At the end, there was a pregnant silence. Then Derek spoke. His voice had lost a little of the formal diplomatic tone.

"I must admit I didn't know the situation was as bad as that. I agree that it is important that something is done. The fact is that you have taken on only one orphanage and there are many, many more. But if at least we can deal with this one, it is one less. I am tied in what I can do but I promise I'll stretch the rules as much as I can to help."

He seemed genuinely moved.

Then he clicked back into the mould.

"Let me give you some details of what H.M Government is at present discussing with the Romanians. When you know these you can drop into the conversation one or two points that could be taken as possible problems for the Romanians if they don't comply."

He then proceeded to give David details of the aid and economic programmes that were being offered to the Romanians.

"At some time mention Gerald Harvey's name, and refer to him as Gerald."

"Who the heck is Gerald Harvey?"

"He is the Minister who is heading up the H.M. Government team for the discussions. They won't know that you don't know him and the familiar use of his name will frighten them to death. I don't need to spell it out to you how and when you use it. But, to help matters along, we will ensure that our Romanian mole here in the embassy – she is one of the assistants to the receptionist – gets to hear that a certain well connected David Edwards is visiting the Embassy, to sound out how genuine are the responses Gerald has been getting in his talks."

David was impressed.

Derek excused himself for five minutes, during which time David tried hard to recall all that had been said. When Derek returned it was if he had been reading David's mind because as he sat down again he said. "All done. Now, let's go through those programmes again."

It was past 7 o'clock by the time that he had absorbed all the detail and David was glad to accept the suggestion that they broke off for dinner. It was almost as if he had never been away. The conversation was again about 'Twickers' and the forthcoming international. Luckily David had lost his cockney accent in the intervening years, so he didn't sound or feel so out of place. Dinner over, David made his apologies and Derek arranged for the taxi to take him to the hotel. No mention was made of the Embassy Club, which no longer functioned, possible due to the changed environment. The dinner had lasted for some little time and the drinks afterwards had left him a little tired. His plea for an early night was quite acceptable.

Taking his time the following morning he showered and shaved and ambled down to breakfast.

To his surprise he found a buffet laid out with cheese and meat, as well as an array of breads. The memories of the stale bread came rushing back. Shortly before 10:30 he asked the reception if he could call a taxi. It was not a Dacia this time, many of which he had seen before, but a Mercedes, although not the very latest model.

The journey was fairly short, but David was grateful he didn't have to locate the offices himself. He paid the taxi driver, who pointed to a meter to indicate the fare.

Again, he noticed the difference on entering the building – no blanket this time, and it was warm inside. Announcing himself to the receptionist who still didn't jump to attention when he arrived, he was finally met by a middle-aged man who emerged from a corridor leading off alongside the balustrade stairs.

"Mr Edwards? Emunescu. Mr Martin said that you were coming. Please come with me."

David followed him, observing that the walls were still green and cream but also noticing when he entered the nicely furnished office that the desk was not of the stereo plastic topped variety that he had seen on his last visit.

"Please sit yourself down. Would you like something to drink? We tend to have Turkish coffee but I don't think that you are used to that."

This is where David thought he would try some 'one-upmanship'.

"Turkish would be fine."

It worked. Mr Emunescu looked a little taken aback. Then recovering a little, he picked up the telephone and ordered the coffee.

Almost before they had started to talk, the coffee arrived complete with the sugar satchels, which enhance the taste.

"I understand that you wish to arrange a meeting with Mr Constantin. How can I be of assistance?"

"Derek Martin, who sends his kindest regards to you, felt that a pre-meeting might be helpful to get your guidance on which points we should cover in the meeting."

Emunescu looked a little puzzled but his expression changed as David outlined the problems he had met.

"So what we want to achieve is to get the responsibility for the orphanage at Bros to be transferred to the village. We can then deal directly with them and, hopefully, get things on a more satisfactory basis."

"There may difficulties." Emunescu's brow had furrowed. "It depends who it was who appointed Mr Domnescu. Before you have the meeting I suggest that this information needs to be obtained. Whilst Mr Constantin is a very good man," David wondered how much of his back Emunescu was covering in making this statement, "if this is someone very senior to Mr Constantin, he will not be able to do much about it." He paused for a few seconds. "Can you delay your meeting until Monday? By then I may be able to find out this information."

It was now Thursday and David had hoped to return to the village on Friday, but he recognised the value of Mr Emunescu's assistance.

"Yes, perhaps you could set up the meeting for Monday early afternoon and I may then be able to get an evening train back to Bros."

"I will do that and in the meantime I will be in touch through Mr Martin."

By this time Derek had finished his coffee remembering to leave the last half-inch in the cup. Strangely, he rather enjoyed it

Emunescu got up, which was an invitation to finish the meeting.

"I am very grateful for your help Mr Emunescu. I am sure that you would want to see to it that the best came out of the assistance that is being given to the children."

His brows furrowed. "We did not know of the situation, Mr Edwards. I have only recently heard of the conditions. I do not think that I could visit the orphanages. You see I have children of my own." He now had a very embarrassed expression on his face.

"I will do my best and call Mr Martin early on Monday so that we can have the information in your hands by late Monday morning in time for the meeting."

With that he lead David out of the office and back to the reception where he spoke to the girl at the desk. Turning to David he said, "The receptionist will call your taxi and I will be in touch." His handshake was firm.

David watched him leave abruptly, perhaps a reflection of his embarrassment over the matter.

Chapter 6

When David returned to the Embassy he learned that Emunescu had already telephoned Derek Martin and told him what he was trying to arrange.

"I need to tell my crew back at Bros what is happening. I don't have any telephone contacts there so how the hell am I going to let them know that I will not be back until Monday at the earliest"

"Don't worry. We will send a courier on a motorbike to advise them. With the roads still uncluttered he can be there and back in four hours. Who should he contact?"

David gave him the details and described the location of Cati's house.

"Now some good news. As you are staying over the weekend, the Ambassador, has asked if you would join him at our residence in Constanta. Not only will it be a break for you but it is an opportunity to get him fully on our side." David noticed with some pleasure the 'our side'.

"Constanta?" The name rang a bell. Then he remembered that he nearly went there on a plane that never was.

"It is on the coast and now a very pleasant tourist resort. We can get you there tomorrow by lunch time and you can return with the Ambassador on Sunday."

"Well provided I can make use of the visit I will not feel too guilty."

"Believe me, it would be very useful. Sir Christopher, Sir Christopher Smith, is a useful man to have batting for you." Again a public-school expression, but David did not mind. He now knew that Derek was 'batting' for him.

Taking it for granted that all was therefore arranged Derek went on, "So dinner here tonight at about 7. And now I suppose that you would like to go back to the Corinthian to freshen up a bit," and with that he lifted the telephone to call a taxi.

"No, hold on Derek. I think that I would like to walk to the hotel. Get a bit of exercise and all that."

"Fine. We will see you at 7 then."

Derek shook his hand and the secretary accompanied him to the door.

Outside, it all seemed so familiar, the gravel path and the soldiers, still as scruffy as ever at the entrance to the area. Turning left he proceeded down the tree-lined street to the Bulervardue Nicolae Bălcesu. This was now much busier than when he had been there before and the vehicles were more varied, no just Dacis, but other foreign makes.

David was in no hurry and his curiosity pricked him when he came to the Theodore on the left hand side of the road. I wonder if it has changed, he thought, and on impulse he turned into the reception area. It was like turning the clock back 14 years. Even the aspidistras seemed the same. But one thing was different.

"Can I help you sir?"

A uniformed young man in a smart hotel uniform had appeared by his side. About 25 years of age, the age that David was when he lodged here, an accent slightly American, his attentive question was accompanied by a pleasant smile.

"No I was just looking in. I stayed here some time ago."

"Oh, we've had many improvements recently and I think that there are some rooms available, would you like me to make enquiries at the reception?"

Now that really was a change. The last time he had had to drag an offer of accommodation out of them.

"No, thanks though, I already have a hotel room at the Corinthian Palace," and with some embarrassment he extracted himself from the pressured approach and returned to the Boulevard.

Continuing along the Boulevard, he crossed over to the turning for his hotel. On entering he picked up his key but instead of going up to his room, he decided, as it was still light and warm, to go out on to the terrace at the back of the hotel.

Seating himself, he caught the attention of one of the waiters and ordered a beer. Surprisingly this arrived fairly promptly and was also pleasantly cold.

Sipping it, he contemplated the past few days and the specific tasks he still had to undertake. He was determined to get the Bros orphanage under the villagers' control. Then he could be sure that further supplies would be put to their proper use.

Still deep in his thought, he was interrupted by an American voice.

"Hi, are you English?" Without waiting for a reply the stranger went on, "I heard you order a beer and I was sure that you were English."

Looking up, David saw that the voice belonged to an American, a bit younger than himself, with crew cut haircut and about 6 foot tall.

"Yes?" David response was enquiring.

"Look, forgive me but I haven't had much contact with English speaking guys since I arrived last week. Can I join you?"

The incident with the other fake American flashed through David's mind and although he felt that history would not repeat itself, he decided to continue with caution.

"Sure, but I won't be here long. I have to go up to my room to get changed shortly for an appointment at the Embassy. Haven't you been to the Embassy Club?"

"Pardon me? What Embassy Club?"

Then David remembered it no longer existed because there was no need for it these days.

"Sorry, there used to be a club for Westerners at the British Embassy in the bad old days."

"The bad old days?"

David explained that he had visited Bucharest during the Communist era.

"Look, I'd better introduce myself." Typical, thought David, how Americans like to give their name and family details on first contact with a stranger, even telling them about their children within minutes of them meeting. English people don't do that. Well, he reflected, both approaches were incomprehensible.

"Bob Dewer, AOS – American Optical Services, one of the biggest ophthalmic and accessories suppliers in the U.S. of A."

David took the proffered hand and gave his name. This was followed by the predictable question.

"So what's your line?"

Trying not to sound too tetchy, David replied , "I'm not actually here on business," and then not wishing to go into detail added, "I'm representing a charitable organisation."

Inevitable it brought on the next question. Sucked into giving further explanation, David told his new companion about the conditions in the orphanages and his involvement in the charity.

Bob listened in silence, a silence that was prolonged for a few moments after David had finished explaining.

"Gee, that's terrible. But somebody has got to do something about it."

Slightly irritated, David replied, "Well, that is why I am here, but it isn't that simple." He went on to explain how he had uncovered the corruption and the disappearance of the aid that had been sent.

Again his companion remained quiet for some time after he had finished.

"Look David, I can call you that can't I? I think AOS may be interested in helping."

Suddenly, David was interested in his companion. "We would be very grateful for any help we can get. We already have American associates working for the Organisation in the States raising funds."

"I wasn't thinking of money. To be honest you can often throw money at something and all it does is drop into the wrong pockets."

"Tell me about it."

"Are you going to be around tomorrow?"

"Only early on." David felt that it was a bit too ostentatious to name drop that he was meeting the British Ambassador.

"How about having breakfast together here, say, 7.00?"

A bit early, David thought, but if something could come out of it he was willing to be there.

"OK Bob." Now he was doing it – first name terms.

"O.K. Now lets see, 5 o'clock here, that's about 9 a.m. Central American Time, yeah just about the right time to catch the company Vice President. So I will see you at breakfast then?" There was a sudden urgency in his voice and he got up to go.

David shook his hand and nodded, settling back to finish the beer that had become slightly warm.

Freshly showered, David made his way to the embassy, returning by the same route.

Deep in thought, he turned into the road leading to the Embassy, remembering his previous visits. A sudden flash back to his experience with Carol crossed his mind. Enjoying the memory of his time with Carol, he wondered where she was now. He remembered how he was so anxious that he kept his socks on. But Carol was only one of the 'Jack-the lad' relationships he had had when he was single. In the end it was Sheila who had triumphed in 'pinning him down', something he now applauded.

How lucky he was to have a settled family and children that have parents, unlike the Romanian children.

The door of the Embassy opened as he arrived and Derek Martin was there to greet him.

"C'mon in old chap. Dinner's nearly ready." He was led to the large dining room where a number of the staff, many of whom he had already met, were already gathered, taking drinks from a small bar in the corner.

"'You remember 'this one' and 'you met' that one 'last night'." The names were rather going over his head but everyone was very welcoming.

The meal was good, a soup and then a lamb dish, lamb being rather a delicacy in Romania where pork was the usual meat. This was followed by an apple crumble and then cheese and biscuits.

The wine was good and a brandy followed it.

"The Ambassador is looking forward to meeting you and hearing of the organisation." Derek was very attentive as on the previous night.

"I hope that we can get his backing."

"Oh I am sure of it."

Then David told Derek all about his meeting with Bob Dewer.

"AOS! Well that's a turn up for the book. They're one of the biggest ophthalmic services company in the States. And word has it that they are in heavy negotiations here to set up a manufacturing base in Romania with Rx houses all over Eastern Europe."

"Rx houses?"

"Prescription lens grinding and lens fitting units serving opticians in all the Central European countries. It will provide massive employment opportunities in Romania if it goes ahead. Romania has been working very hard to stop it going to Hungary. And you say that this Bob Dewer..?""

"Yes, Bob Dewer."

"..is interested in the orphanage problem?"

"Well, he appeared to be, but I will know more about the extent of his interest at breakfast tomorrow."

"I think that you should let Sir Christopher know of the outcome of your breakfast meeting."

Then, relaxing, he moved David on to join the others, who were engaging in the usual small talk about sport and England's chances against Wales. This proved to be more interesting than usual as there was a really patriotic Welshman in the company who was rubbing in past victories in the face of the suggestion that England was going to thrash the Welsh.

Chapter 7

David was down at the breakfast room prompt at 7 a.m. Even so, Bob Dewer was already sitting at one of the tables. When he saw David, he gave a wave.

"Good morning, and how are you this morning?" the greeting was typically American but never the less genuine. Seating himself, David ordered coffee and rolls from the waiter who approached almost as his bottom touched the seat. This was certainly a change from the 'old times'.

"Very well, thank you, you must have been up bright and early."

"It's an American habit. In the States we have a lot of breakfast meetings. The reason given is that the mind is supposed to be fresher at that time of the day and meeting periods are not productive times. Really that is a load of bullshit. It really comes down to the demonstration of power by the boss, making his guys toe the line and jump when he tells them to."

David thought it refreshing that Bob could criticise the American way of life that he himself often found ostentatious.

"Now," continued Bob, "I spoke with Al, Al Wagner, Vice President, last night, and he wants in."

"I'm sorry?"

"He wants in, – part of the action." Then, seeing the continued blank look on David's face. Bob went on to explain that he had had a long telephone call with this Al and recounted the details about the orphanage that David had given him the previous night.

"He's got kids, you know, and firstly he wants your contact name in the States."

David explained that he could put Lucy in touch with him.

"And I am to give you any help I can to get your immediate problem resolved."

"Well, that's great, but I do not know how you can help."

"David, are you listening to me?" the bluntness rather took him aback.

"AOS have still to sign the co-operation agreement for our plant here. Al has authorised me to tell the Romanians to stuff their agreement up their arsehole if they are not prepared to co-operate fully with you on the orphanage at, where was it, Bloss?"

"Bros," corrected David still reeling at the turn of events.

"So when are you seeing the guy Constantin?"

"On Monday morning."

"Then be prepared for some sort of initial reluctance, the guy has to save his face, but," and there was a pause, "he will arrange to draw up a full authorisation for the villages to take over the control before you leave in the afternoon, believe me."

David could hardly believe what he was hearing.

"And," continued Bob "since AOS is now part of the Organisation, we want to be in on the other plans, OK?"

"Bob, what can I say? Obviously thanks is not enough but if all you say comes about, you will certainly have played an important part in getting the plight of the children improved."

"Now, I must dash. My meeting is at 8.30 and I will enjoy seeing the bastards squirm. Here's my card. Get your Lucy to get in touch sometime next week when I am back in the States. And on the next visit I want to go up to Bloss," he correct himself, "Bros."

With that Bob grabbed David's hand and, with a broad smile, turned and hurried out.

Still sitting there, David reflected on what Bob had told him. If it all came about it could be a dramatic move forward. He went on to mull over the proposed meeting with the Ambassador. Should he take up the opportunity or leave it until he saw the outcome of his meeting with Constantin?

To his surprise he began to think in political terms. If he saw the Ambassador and Bob's pressure did have the right effect, the satisfactory outcome could be credited to the Ambassador, what ever he did or didn't do. That could be a good thing as it would tie the Ambassador to the campaign.

Rather pleased with himself, David returned to his room for his overnight bag and set off for the Embassy.

When he arrived at the Embassy gates he was surprised to see a Jaguar in the forecourt with a uniformed chauffer busy polishing the bonnet. The door of the Embassy opened and a smartly dressed man of about 40 stepped forward.

'Saw you coming. Peter Davis." He thrust out his hand. "'Tis David isn't it? Derek said that you would be prompt." And with that he grabbed David's bag and ushered him into the Jaguar; the rear doors had already been opened by the chauffeur.

"We have a bit of a ride to Constanta but Sir Christopher is looking forward to meeting you." He nodded to the chauffeur who moved round to take up the driving seat and began to ease the Jaguar out of the Embassy courtyard into the side road and then into the Boulevard. The smoothness of the ride impressed him and for a moment he was absorbed by the luxury of the experience of travelling in a Jaguar.

"From what Derek Martin has told me, you really have been busy since you've been back. When was it you were here before?"

"Mid 1970s, during Ceauşescu's time."

"I know of it but I was in the States at that time. I understand it was pretty awful." A bit of an understatement, David thought. "But nothing could be done at that time, I understand, about the orphanages." At that point David realised that he had matured over the years. Earlier he would have blown up at that comment instead of which he said nothing. "Still, with things now different, hopefully Sir Christopher can drop the right remarks in the right places to give you some assistance."

The conversation after that became general; Peter asking what David did back home and how he saw the forthcoming Olympic Games coming out as far as Great Britain was concerned. He was obviously a professional in public relations and David decided to play along with him. He was a pleasant bloke, anyway.

The journey, which David estimated was about 200 kilometres took some three hours, the Jaguar reached speeds of 90 miles per hour in some places, but seemed to be gliding at only 40. For some of the time they discussed the development of Romania, coming to the joint conclusion that the country still had a long way to go to catch up with western systems and democracy. David noticed that Peter was careful to avoid associating himself directly with any comments, instead using such phrases as 'they say' and 'it is thought that'. Typical of a diplomat, David thought. Nevertheless, he was well informed and David enjoyed their discussion of the broad Romanian situation.

As they approached Constanta, David was able to see that the buildings were different from those of Bucharest. Here they were less ornate and of a later period. There was still an impression of the 1920s about them, he thought, but the spaciousness between buildings was very noticeable. He likened it a little to the more opulent Bournemouth, rather than Southend-on-Sea, which was the seaside resort that he had often visited as a teenager and in his early twenties.

The Jaguar had slowed down now and they could see the sea front. The car turned down a road parallel to what David assumed was the promenade, turned into some gates fronted by a Romanian soldier, and came finally to rest in front of a large house. The chauffer was quick to jump out and opened the door for David almost as soon as they had stopped. Peter was left to let himself out, but quickly came round to help David out.

"C'mon old man let's go and meet his nibs," he commented, gently ushering David to the large door, whilst the chauffeur followed on with David's overnight bag.

The door opened and a young man greeted him.

"Good afternoon Mr Edwards. I hope that you had a pleasant journey. Perhaps I can show you to your room and you can freshen up before you meet Sir Christopher. He is looking forward to meeting you." That phrase again. With that the young man led the way to a wide staircase opposite the door and at the top turned right, past some portraits of people who David didn't recognise, to the second door on the right. Entering, the young man stood aside for David to go in. To say that the room was sumptuous would be an understatement.

The furnishing were antique and obviously of very high quality. The large bed with a silken cover was like those that David had had seen only in films. To the right were French doors already open to a small balcony from which was a view over the sea.

"I'm sure that you will be comfortable, and the bathroom is here." He opened a door to the left revealing a large marble-lined bathroom, complete with a deep bath and gold taps. "When you are ready, please come down and I can take you into the drawing room where Sir Christopher is looking forward to meeting you." If I hear that once more thought David, I'll scream.

David thought he would feel a little guilty enjoying the luxury over the weekend, but if it achieved the objective he felt that he could justify the visit.

Having laid out his toilet things and washed his face and hands and combed his hair, he felt tidy enough to meet the Ambassador.

Venturing out of the room, he proceeded down the staircase to be met by the young man again, Peter seemed to have disappeared.

"Everything comfortable for you?" and without waiting for an answer he was led down the corridor to a large solid oak door on the left. Opening it, the young man stood aside for David to enter. The room was large and furnished with a large antique desk and a number of leather armchairs. On one side stood a cabinet, which David took to be a drinks repository.

Standing by the French doors facing out of the room was a silver-haired figure. He turned and approached David, and in an unexpected Scottish accent addressed him with "Come in laddy, sit yer'self down," indicating one of the leather armchairs. A bit taken back, all that David could do was say, "Good afternoon Sir Christopher," and then, recovering a little, he moved to the chair, reluctant to sit while his host was still standing.

Perhaps realising the situation, Sir Christopher moved to the chair beside him and indicated that they should both sit down.

"I have been looking forward to meeting you." So it was true. "I've been hearing what you are doing and am very impressed with what you are trying to achieve." The accent wasn't polished, not even Edinburgh, could even have been Glaswegian. "I believe you were here in the 1970s?"

"I was representing a firm of agents who had principles engaged in business with the Romanians at that time. In fact I still work with one of them, Krone Chemicals, but only in the UK."

"They were difficult times weren't they?" He spoke as if he knew something about the period and, seeing David's questioning expression, continued, "Oh yes, I was here at that time too, laddy, I was a sales director with one of the divisions of Thompson Electric, that was before they were taken over by GEC. We were hoping to get some work on the generating side but it all came to nothing in the end. When I now think of the time wasted and all the intrigue we had to suffer I wonder how we stood it."

As if to answer the unanswered question, he went on, "That is how I got this job, if you can call it a job. I still find it a bit frustrating having to work with the professional civil servants. Oh, they're all right in their way but they've never seen the real world like you and me. They wouldn't know where to put their face on hearing the passion and language on the cop at the Rangers ground. You know, Twickers is all right but the punch ups there are only on the pitch." His laughter was infectious.

"It was because I had been here at that time that, having retired from my own business and got the knighthood for my charity work, I was asked to take on the post. And I can tell you that some things haven't changed. The corruption is still there, even more obvious now."

He got up and went over to the cabinet and drew down the front; it was, as David had thought, a drinks cabinet.

"I know the sun's not over the yard arm yet, but because you are a guest I can indulge myself. What would you like, whiskey, gin, sherry…?"

"If there is a beer there I wouldn't say no." This produced a nod and a can of Bass was pressed into his hand, followed by a glass. Pouring a good measure of Scotch, Sir Christopher returned to his seat.

"Now we have a good two hours before dinner, put me in the picture on what happened when you were here, how you got into this and what you have achieved or, for that matter, not achieved so far. The latter is where, hopefully I might be able to play some part."

With this he settled down expectantly into the depth of the armchair.

David readily obliged and was encouraged with nods when he recounted the sights that he'd seen during his first visit. There was silence as he explained how, following his return to England, he had involved himself with building up international connections and raising funds to send relief supplies out to Romania.

He couldn't hide his anger when he related what had happened to their donations and his determination to get the control of the orphanages out of corrupt hands.

Sir Christopher, who had remained intently silent during this time, slowly got up and walked to the drinks cabinet and refilled his glass.

"You were fortunate in a way. When I was here, although the embassy knew of the orphanages, they never spoke to anybody about them. They ignored the problem and I was angry when I first found out about this. Now I have come to realise that there was nothing that they could have done about them. Ceauşescu was unapproachable and business with Romania was too important to be disturbed by intervention into domestic policies."

He sat down again at this point. "You discovered the orphanage, so then they had to own up to knowing about them. But now...." he paused, "we should do something but, as I said, very little has changed. Business is still an important issue and many of Ceauşescu's top people are still in power."

Although David had learnt a little patience as he got older, he could feel his anger beginning to rise. Was this wretched official going to do nothing, just like the others?

He was just saved from the embarrassment of lambasting his host, as Sir Christopher went on.

"At least that is what the Foreign Office want us to do. But quite frankly, David, I don't care a shit what they want. They want me here so that I can oil a few wheels, but I can ruffle a few feathers too. You mentioned to Derek Martin that you had met this laddy from AOS, Bob Stewart?"

"Bob Dewer," David corrected.

"Bob Dewer. We know of the AOS company. They have branches in the UK – large company based in Connecticut, USA. Who did he say the Vice President was?"

David thought. "He said Al something. Al Wallace, Walter .. no.."

"It's Al Wagner," interrupted Sir Christopher. "He headed up the UK company called BAOS, British American Ophthalmic Society in Slough in the 1960s. From what I remember from comments about him he was a nice chap, a wee bit prone to like his food, but very happy to be in the UK. We know of their intention to set up an Eastern European network of Rx houses. We don't have anything international in that line in the UK so we have no conflict of interest." He paused and David thought it better not to say anything just yet.

Suddenly Sir Christopher looked at his watch. And then looked into space for a full minute.

"When did you say Bob…. Dewer is meeting Constantin?"

"Monday morning." Again a pause looking to the ceiling.

Then, with a turn of speed belying his age and silvery head, he dashed to his desk and pressed a bell.

Almost immediately the young man who had greeted David came in armed with a notebook.

"Roger, I want to send a note to Derek Martin and I want it to go open so that our Romanian mole can get wind of it. O.K.? Ready?"

Roger had seated himself at the adjoining table to the desk, notebook at the ready.

Sir Christopher started dictating.

"'Urgent. Confidential. Derek Martin stop. We understand that the representative of AOS is in Bucharest. Can you try to contact him and invite him to meet me at Bucharest on Monday afternoon to discuss possible merger with UK company wishing to set up network of Rx houses based in Prague. Other details will be disclosed when we meet. Signed Christopher'. Got that? Right, off you go, laddy."

No sooner had Roger left than he picked up the telephone.

"Get me Derek Martin at Bucharest please."

There was a slight delay then Sir Christopher started to speak. "Hello Derek, Christopher here. What odds are you giving me on us thrashing you at Murreyfield tomorrow? ...come on, you ought to have more confidence that that. O.K. I'll accept a bottle of malt to a bottle of gin. Now I have just sent you a note. I want you to ignore it but see that our Romanian mole gets it a wee bit quickly. It concerns David's problem. Hopefully Constantin will get the information later today and it could help matters along. You'll see the idea when you read it. Bye, oh, and by the way, send the malt up by courier." He laughed that belly laugh again.

Turning to David, Sir Christopher said, "David, when Derek Martin sent you up here he was going through the motions. Nice a laddy as he is, he wants, as everyone in the diplomatic service does, to cover his arse. He knew that I and, in fact, the British Government are powerless to do anything about your problem face to face. There is still big business and politics involved. However, to give him his due, he does know what a cunning Scottish sod I can be and was perhaps clinging to the hope that I might do something that a professional diplomat wouldn't dream of doing. And I have." He laughed again.

"When our mole in the embassy, who unknowingly is very useful when we want to leak something, gets that information he will pass it on and, just like the old times, it will be passed to the department negotiating with AOS. Hopefully, when Bob Dewer puts the screws on they will think that there is a simple alternative to locating the Rx head quarters in Romania and not procrastinate over his demands." He smiled smugly.

David could see that his journey had not been in vain.

"Thank you very much Sir Christopher. If it all comes off, I will see that you get a bottle of Malt from me on our next visit."

"Save your money for the cause. Let's hope that this orphanage can come under the control of the village. From what you say they seem nice people. I never got out of Bucharest when I was here so I never had the chance to find out what those not directly under the control of the system were like. And although I fancied a few of the darker sex I met, there was no opportunity to get one's leg over." again the laugh.

David thought, if only he knew.

"Now tell me about the international organisation, and your future plans."

Without realising it, David went on for at least half an hour, encouraged by the good listener sitting opposite him. Suddenly embarrassed, he apologised for going on for so long.

"Not at all. I find it very interesting and, before you go, I'll give you a few names you might find useful back in the UK. Now lets break off so that you can rest a little before dinner at, say seven?"

David nodded and excused himself, finding his way back to his room. He was very excited about what might develop from his visit.

Dinner was a pleasant affair, the small staff at the villa all ate with Sir Christopher and, although they deferred to him, as was perhaps required, they obviously felt relaxed in his company. Enjoying having a compatriot of the Ceauşescu times, Sir Christopher recounted some of his experiences, which mirrored, in many ways, those of David's.

In concurring with some of these experiences David found himself the centre of attention at times. That, and the wine, combined to make a very pleasant evening.

The meal over and the chat finished, Sir Christopher excused himself, but invited David to join him in the lounge where he poured two large glasses of brandy.

Accepting one of these and also the comfortable armchair, David reflected that it hadn't all been hard graft.

"You know David, you will still have a lot of hard work trying to get the orphanage business sorted out. Unfortunately, unlike Hungary, which I also visited during my sales days, Romania has not cleared out the old guard and, as I said, there is now a lot of corruption. Ceauşescu was an evil man but under him nobody fiddled. Now they all do it. But you've made a good start and, within my cunning little world, I will do everything I can to help, but you have to recognise that you cannot rely upon this or any other government to do much. There is too much politics involved."

They chatted on for a little while but David could see that his host was getting tired.

"If you don't mind, Sir Christopher, I think that I will slip off to bed."

"You do that laddy and sleep well. Breakfast is at 9 o'clock tomorrow, then after that our ways part. You back to Bucharest after you've been taken round the resort and I'm straight off on a flight back to the UK. I'd give you a lift in the helicopter but policy, that stupid red tape, prevents it. Good night David, sleep well."

Following a sumptuous breakfast of bacon and eggs followed by hot rolls and marmalade, David said farewell to St Christopher and watched him walk out across the lawn to board the helicopter.

As the detritus of breakfast was being cleared away, Roger, the young P.A. to Sir Christopher, came in.

"The old man would like you to see a little of the resort before your leave, so I thought that we would take an hour or so driving around and stop off at a café before you are taken in the car back to Bucharest."

"That's very kind of you, if it is no trouble."

"No trouble at all," and he indicated that they should go in the same Jaguar that had brought David to Constanta.

The tour was an eye opener for David. The wide sandy beaches were inviting and he could see the ribbon development of the new hotels on the front was emulating that of English seaside towns, although the buildings were still Eastern European in style.

"It has always been a fairly smart resort, but only reserved for the elite," commented Roger.

They stopped off at a café on the sea front; the thing that David noticed most was that the tablecloths were starched and not the limp versions that he had seen during his first visit. Roger ordered in Romanian. Coffee, not Turkish, arrived together with a small glass of a pale coloured drink.

"It is a Romanian additive to the coffee," Roger explained smiling, "it should be drunk down quickly before the coffee."

David tried it and felt a warm glow with an almond taste. This was accentuated when he took his first sip of the coffee.

He commented warmly on this and Roger seemed pleased. After about an hour and a half they returned to the Villa. David was surprised to find his overnight back in the hallway. Shaking hands, Roger explained, "It has all been packed for you. And now I hope that you have enjoyed your stay and will enjoy the ride back."

Settling back he cast mind over the whole trip and felt that it had been not only very worthwhile, but very pleasant, not to say illuminating.

Chapter 8

When David checked back in the Corinthian Palace hotel, a message had been left for him to call at the Embassy at eleven the next morning. Having spent a quiet evening at the hotel and taken an early night, the following morning David tensely awaited the meeting with Constantin later in the day. So, after an early breakfast, he strolled slowly round to arrive at the Embassy a little before eleven.

He was answered at the entrance by the receptionist, who he had met before, and taken along to see Derek Martin who immediately jumped up from his desk and came round to greet him.

"Hello David." His welcome seemed very genuine.

"I wanted to check that all went well and to tell you that we followed the 'ole man's instruction. The information will have got through by now, so Constantin will know, or think that he knows, that if he fails to get the AOS deal finalised this morning it is likely to go to the Czech republic. What did you think of the 'ole man?"

"I was very impressed, he seems to be very sharp."

"He's a bit of a rough diamond but he certainly is that. He's pulled quite a few stunts like this one and been very successful. Let's hope his success rate doesn't falter. Incidentally Emunescu has been back and apparently there is no one above Constantin who is likely to interfere with his decision."

"Derek, if all goes well, I need to get on the evening train back to Bros. Can you arrange tickets etc."

"Consider it done and I am sure that you won't have any need to hang around. Come and have a snack lunch so that you can go straight to the station after your meeting. I can then arrange for a car to take you to the Cultural Offices. It will add to your status if you arrive in an embassy car."

With that he lead the way to one of the reception rooms that David had been in before and had a light snack from a well laid out cold buffet. The two of them chatted on a little, then David took his leave and found the embassy car waiting outside, complete with flying banner on the bonnet.

The offices were the other side of the boulevard, located alongside the Intercontinental Hotel. As soon as David entered, an attractive receptionist dressed in a pale blue blouse and navy skirt got up from her small desk. Although well aware of his married status he couldn't help noticing that she was pretty and well proportioned. If only there had been this freedom when he was here last, he would have willingly invited this one back to his hotel. Back down to earth, he said to her, "David Edwards for Mr Constantin."

"Yes sir. Please take a seat."

His mind drifted back to his reception at the Tourist offices some 14 years earlier when he had to demand attention from the girl to sort out his accommodation. Things had changed, but not as much as he had expected.

The receptionist had disappeared, but now returned and with a winning smile, beckoned him to follow her.

He was taken along the corridor and invited to enter through a large door on the left.

Sitting behind a large desk was a middle-aged man, not unlike Mr Deiter, the pseudo General Manager who had tried to entrap him into an involvement in the Golescu affair. He could well imagine that here was one who had slipped the net and was back in power.

"Mr Edwards. Please come in and sit down." The smile was fixed and blatantly false. David sat in an armchair.

"I understand that you want to discuss the orphanage at Bros. It is my understanding that Domnescu is not performing his function very well."

"Mr Constantin, what you understand is totally wrong. He is performing his function very well, if that function is to siphon off the funds that have been sent here for improvements, or is it possible that these have been diverted to some one in the Cultural office?"

Constantin turned a little pale. "I cannot believe that that is the situation, although I did have some misgivings when he was appointed. I will do my utmost to see that his performance improves."

"No, Mr Constantin. Your 'misgivings' were right, he is totally unsuitable for the position. It is also obvious that central administration of the orphanage is not the best way to achieve improvements. I had the opportunity to discuss the situation with Gerald, Gerald Harvey, just before I left the UK and he agreed with me that local management is by far the best way of getting things done. I would like to see, Mr Constantin, Mr Domnescu removed and you to make an official appointment of the Bros Village as the administrators of the Bros Orphanage."

"Well, that is a possibility. I will give that some thought."

"No, Mr Constantin, before I leave today I want your signed dismissal notice of Domnescu and a letter authorising the village to take over the orphanage immediately."

For a moment, David thought he had gone too far. Constantin appeared to stiffen then quite noticeable dropped his shoulders.

"Mr Harvey is due to meet up with our Trade Development people the week after next. Will you be seeing him before he leaves the UK?"

"I have a meeting with him when I return next week on many matters." David had never lied so blatantly before.

"I wonder if I could leave you for a minute so that I can make some appropriate arrangements? My secretary can get you something to drink while you're waiting?"

"That would be nice. Turkish coffee please."

Not the end but (hopefully) the beginning of the end....